SCROLL SAW PATTERN BOOK

Patrick Spielman & Patricia Spielman

Sterling Publishing Co., Inc.   New York

DEDICATION

To Robert, Sherri, and Sandra, our son and daughters, who also appreciate fine woodworking.

Library of Congress Cataloging-in-Publication Data

Spielman, Patrick E.
    Scroll saw pattern book.

    Includes index.
    1. Jig saws.   2. Woodwork.   I. Spielman, Patricia.
II. Title.
TT186.S674   1986   745.51   86-14358
ISBN 0-8069-4772-1 (pbk.)

            7   9   10   8   6

Copyright © by Patrick and Patricia Spielman
Published by Sterling Publishing Co., Inc.
Two Park Avenue, New York, N.Y. 10016
Distributed in Canada by Oak Tree Press Ltd.
% Canadian Manda Group, P.O. Box 920, Station U
Toronto, Ontario, Canada M8Z 5P9
Distributed in the United Kingdom by Blandford Press
Link House, West Street, Poole, Dorset BH15 1LL, England
Distributed in Australia by Capricorn Ltd.
P.O. Box 665, Lane Cove, SW 2066
Manufactured in the United States of America
All rights reserved

Table of Contents

ACKNOWLEDGMENTS

We thank Walter Schutz for providing us with some good design ideas. The silhouette patterns on pages 186–191 are adaptations of designs from his collection of scroll sawings made by an unknown New York artist. Thanks to Sherri Spielman for her help with the project painting and photography. We especially prize the designs and cutouts perfected by our son, Bob Spielman, which have become some of our most popular projects.

Finally, we express our sincerest gratitude to our friend and employee, Julie Kiehnau, who expertly cut out many of the test projects and other designs. Her speed and skill with a scroll saw are especially valued, as are her excellent typing and "store-keeping" abilities.

Patrick and Patricia Spielman
Spielmans Wood Works

Introduction

One of the problems common to all scroll-saw users is the difficulty of finding good, inexpensive, and easy-to-copy project patterns. It is with this in mind and the urging of magazine and book editors, scroll-saw manufacturers, and our woodworking friends that we have assembled this book of patterns.

This selection of over 450 designs includes ideas for making household accessories such as wall plaques, pegboards, candle holders, and ornaments. Also included are many of the currently popular "country cutouts," puzzles, and projects incorporating the always delightful heart design. (Someone once told us, "If you want it to sell, put a heart on it." That bit of advice has proven to be true.)

There are many great projects in this selection that are easy for the beginner to make successfully. There are also a good number of somewhat-more-complex patterns intended for the experienced craftsperson and hobbyist. Many of the basic patterns are ideal for those individuals who enjoy woodburning (Illus. 1), painting (Illus. 2), stencilling, applying decals, and/or adding other individual touches. These decorative accents create beautiful household accessories and make great gifts. (Incidentally, a soft-tip marker [Illus. 3] can sometimes be used to color wood cutouts,

but remember, it has a tendency to bleed on some softwoods.) The different ways of implementing these patterns into completed projects are limited only by the imagination.

A scroll saw is the only tool needed to complete most of the projects. However, some also require the use of a hand or electric drill. It should also be noted that many of the designs and patterns here can also be cut out with a band saw.

Several full-size alphabets and number patterns are included. These will be useful for making wooden signs, nameplates, and house numbers. If you are interested in making wood signs, two books worth reading are: *Making Wood Signs* and *Alphabets and Designs for Wood Signs*. Both are published by Sterling Publishing Co.

The advanced craftsperson will find some patterns for fretwork shelves, shelf brackets, picture frames, and compound sawing projects. There is also an abundance of ideas for fancy scroll-saw inlays, segmented pictures, and marquetry designs. Many patterns can be used simply as a starting point for the creative woodworker. If, for example, you need a leaf design for an inlaid jewelry box, you'll find some design ideas here, but you can expand on these designs.

Illus. 1. Some details can be outlined with a woodburning tool.

Illus. 2. You can add a touch of color with craft paint.

Illus. 3. Soft-tip markers can be used to color areas outlined with a woodburning tool.

Although the patterns are what we consider a useable size, we certainly encourage their modification in size or detailing to satisfy individual requirements. Some alternate ways to use the designs and patterns to enhance a specific project are as follows:

1. *Change sizes.* Enlarge or reduce patterns as you see fit. To copy and transfer patterns, do the following: Draw with a ruler small, uniformly sized squares all over transparent tissue paper. These squares should all be either ¼ inch or ½ inch in size. The greater the detail and the smaller the design being copied, the smaller the squares should be drawn. Next, on a large piece of paper, about the size that you want the eventual project design to be, divide the space up with exactly the same number of squares as occupied by the design under the transparent tissue paper. The size of the larger set of squares can also be determined by the enlargement ratio desired. If you want the design twice the size, then draw big squares twice the size of the smaller ones.

Now, copy the design square by square. Copy each point of the original pattern on to the graph squares. Curves may be

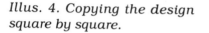

Illus. 4. Copying the design square by square.

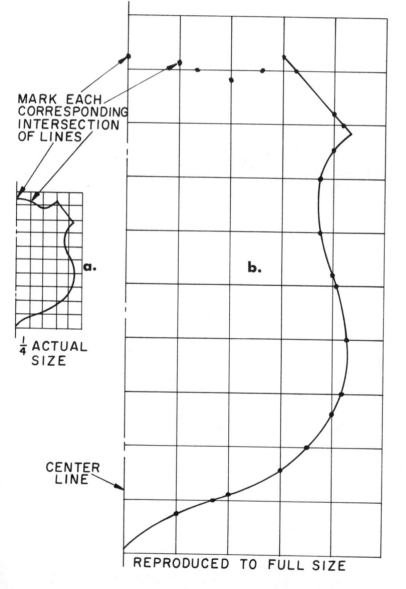

MARK EACH
CORRESPONDING
INTERSECTION
OF LINES

a.

b.

¼ ACTUAL
SIZE

CENTER
LINE

REPRODUCED TO FULL SIZE

drawn by "eye" after locating them with reference to their surrounding square. However, it is more accurate to mark the points where the line of the curve strikes each horizontal and vertical line, as shown in Illus. 4. The example shown has a 1 to 4 ratio, which means the design is enlarged four times larger than the original.

One final point. Some office copy machines have enlargement and reduction capabilities.

2. *Flop the design.* If a goose faces one way, just reverse it, or use two facing each other.

3. *Use the design in multiples.* For example, a row of pigs (connected or not) might be more interesting than just one, single pig.

4. *Crop the design.* Use only a part of it. For example, using just the head of a dog from a pattern might be more appropriate for your needs than a full-bodied pattern.

5. *Change the intended purpose.* Instead of using a pig puzzle design, for example, as a puzzle, drill holes in the back to convert it into a crayon holder or just drill a single hole to make it into a country candle holder.

6. *Paint some, stain some, do not put a finish on some projects.* Different finishes and colors applied to the same project suggest variety, which is important if you are selling your scroll-saw cutouts.

If you are new to scroll sawing or you anticipate buying a scroll saw, we recommend our companion book, the *Scroll Saw Handbook*, also published by Sterling Publishing Co. It contains all of the necessary information on using scroll saws, including descriptions and illustrations of the major kinds of scroll saws and explorations of the special features and limitations of the various machines. Also included are chapters on blade selection, basic sawing skills, bevel sawing, inlay work, compound sawing, marquetry, and many more areas of scroll-saw use. The advice, ideas, and tips presented in the *Scroll Saw Handbook* will help turn you into a skilled scroll-saw operator.

We hope that this book, the *Scroll Saw Pattern Book*, will provide you with many enjoyable hours of making scroll-saw projects, and that you will find enough ideas to keep you always looking forward to the next, new project.

Patrick and Patricia Spielman

Country Cutouts

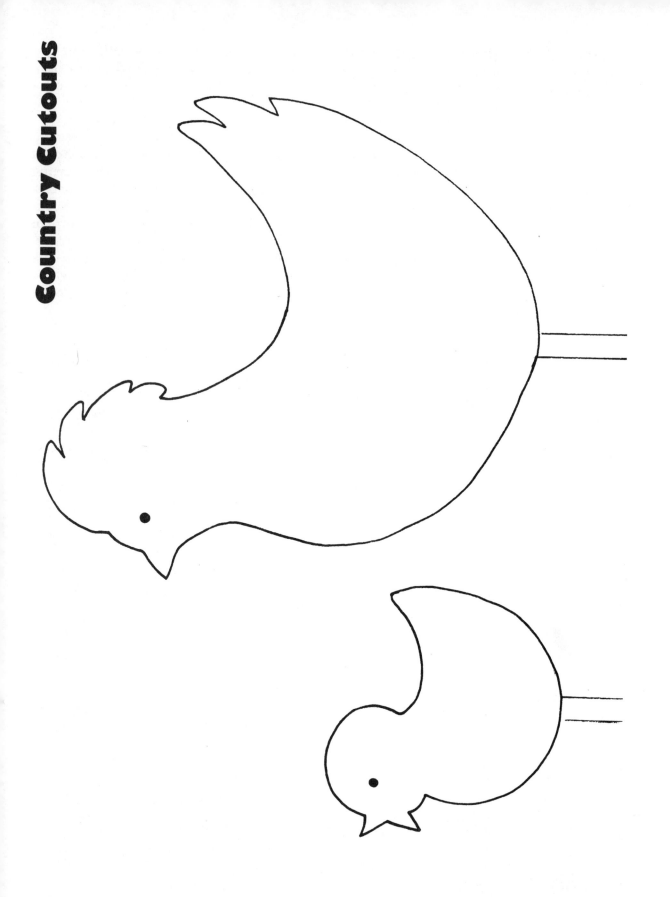

Country cutouts (above and below).

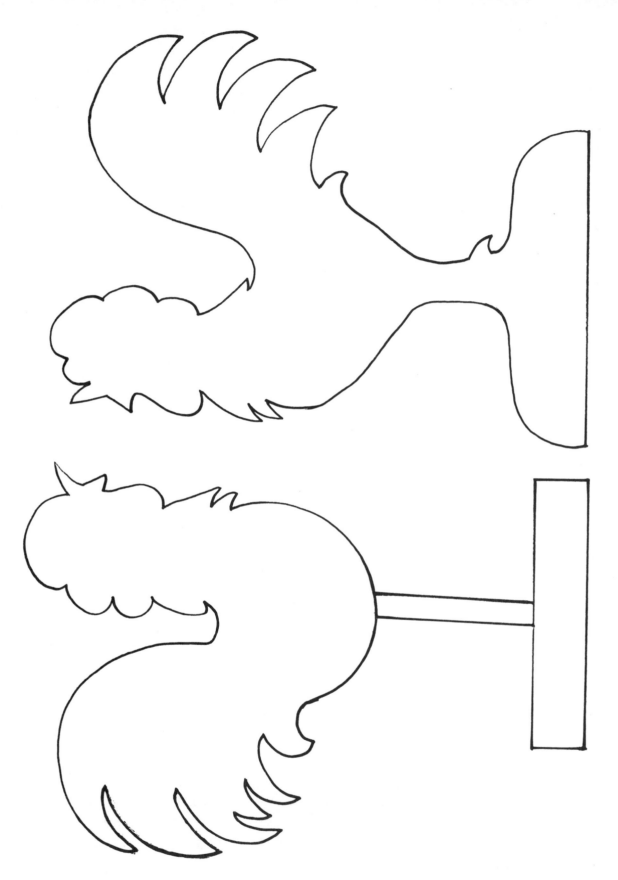

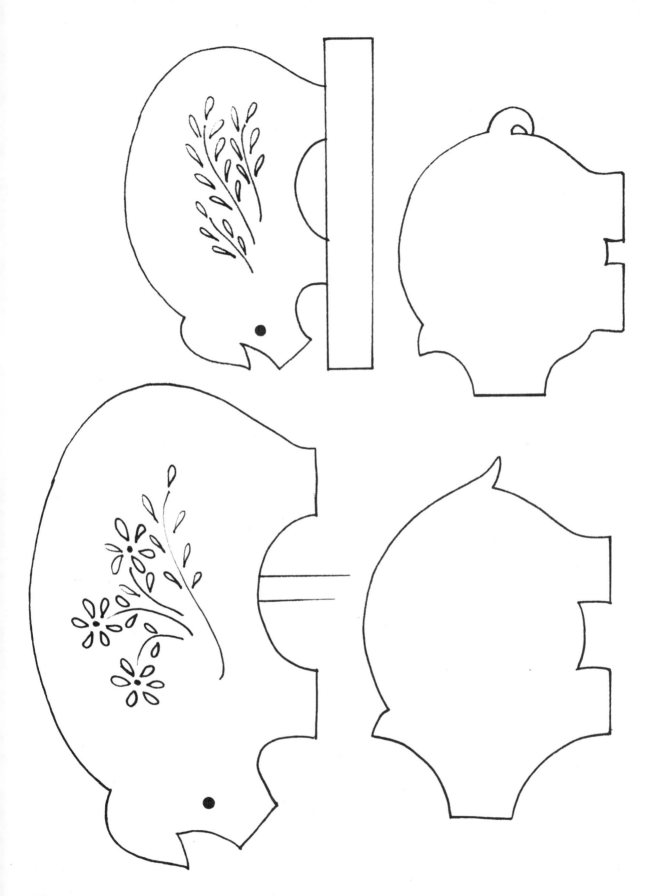

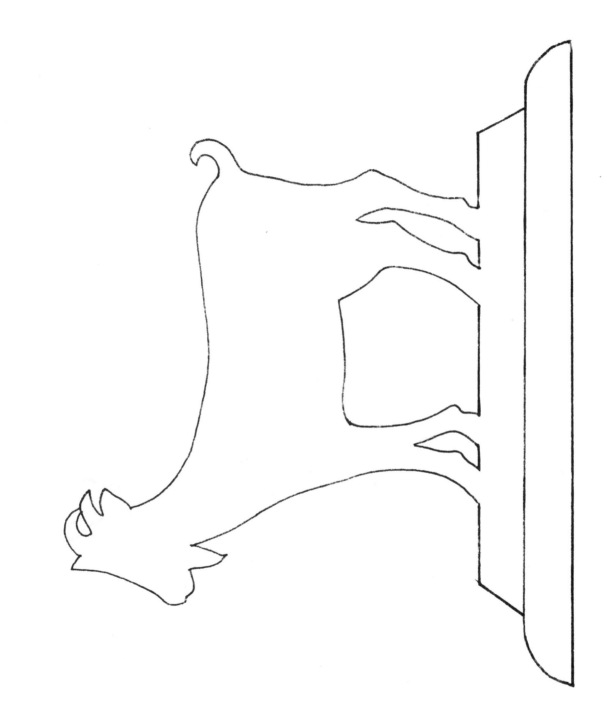

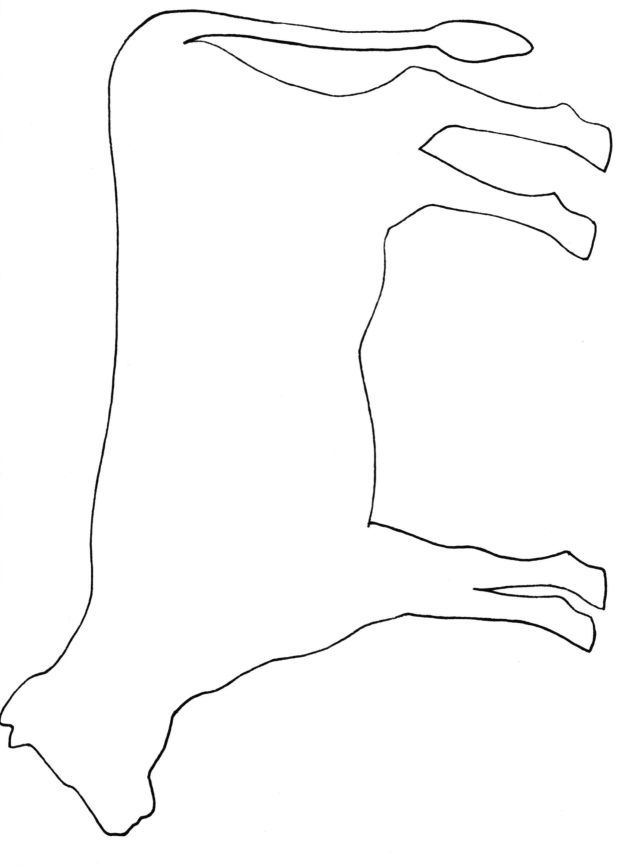

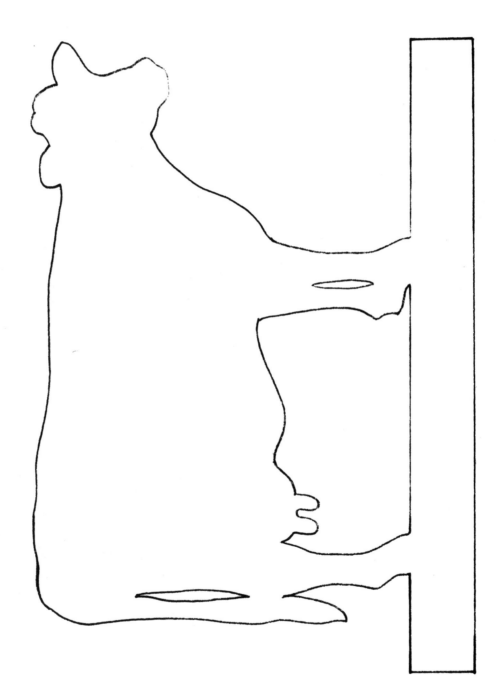

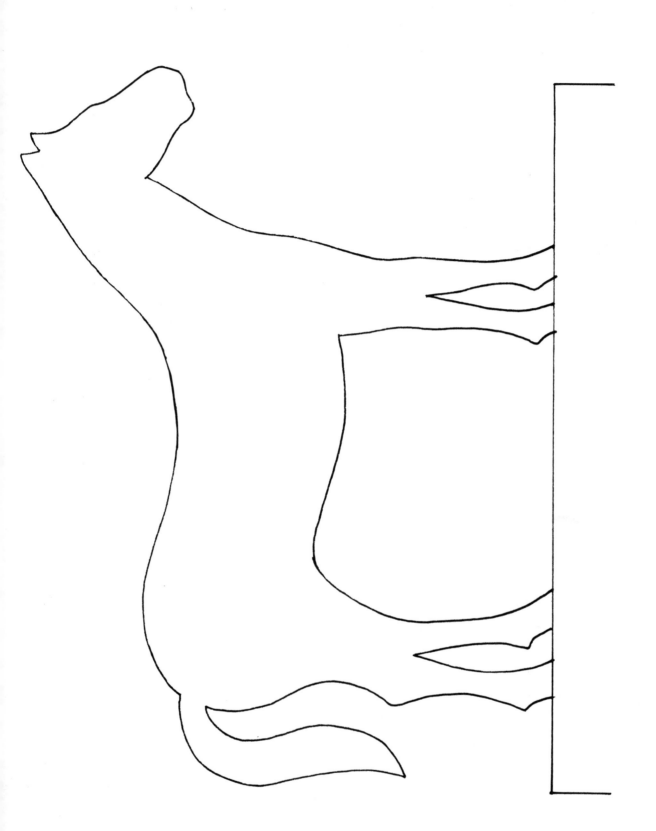

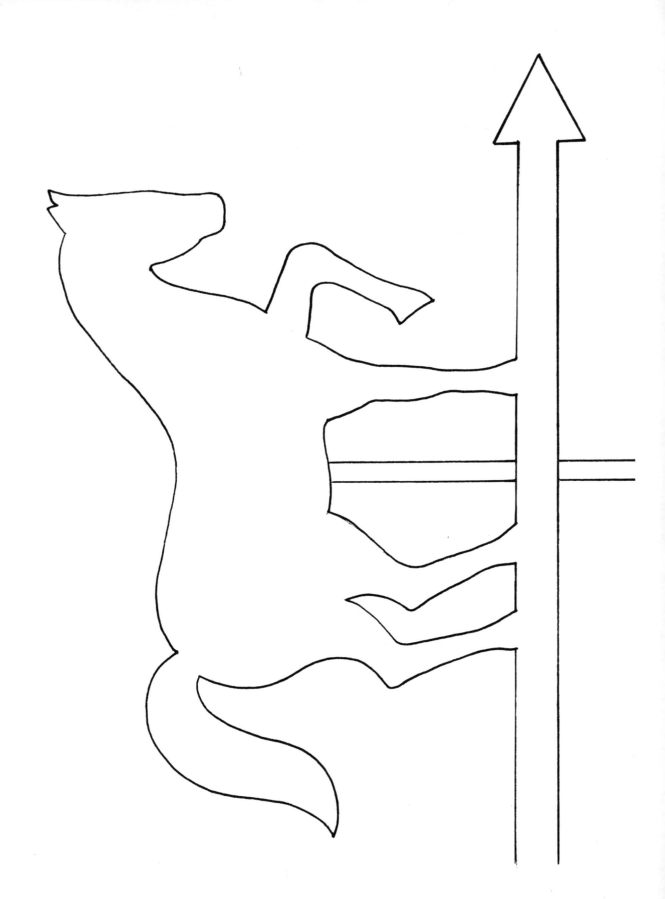

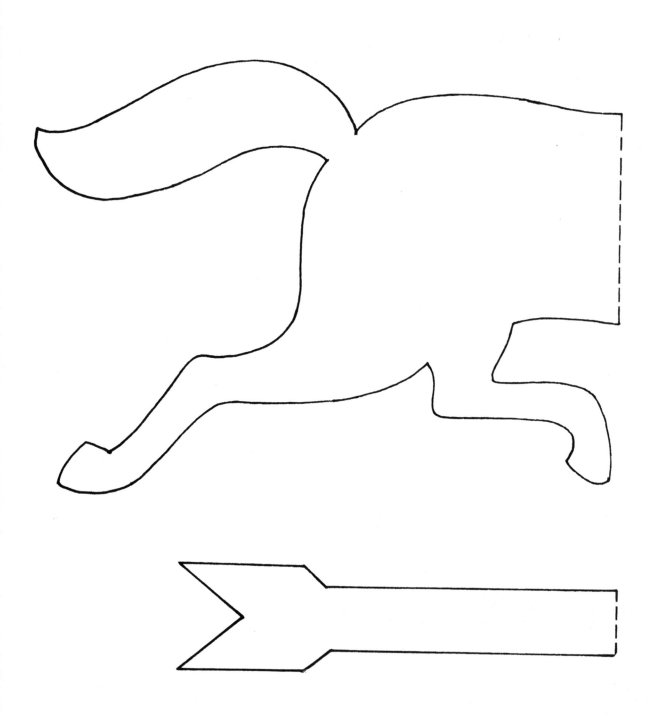

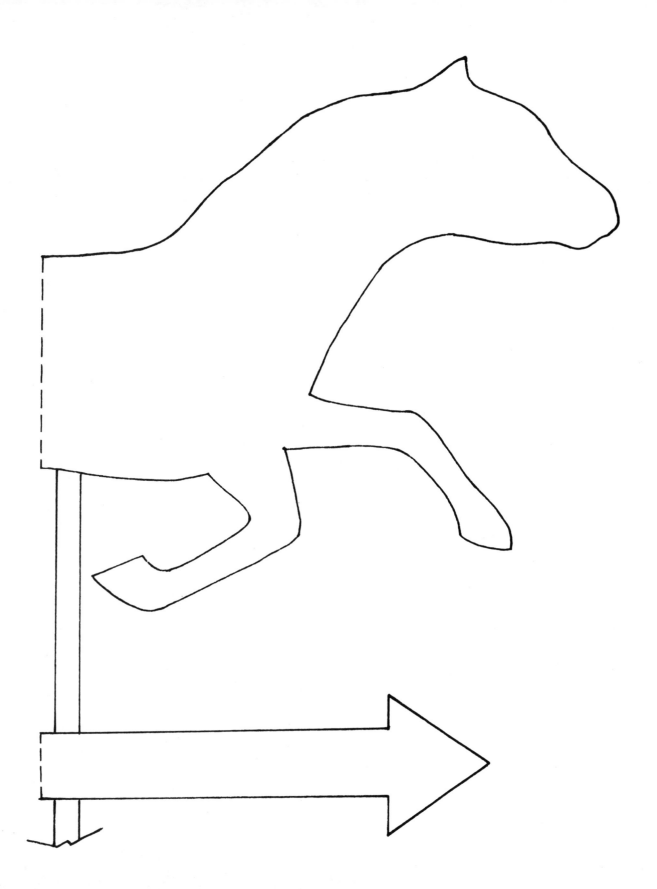

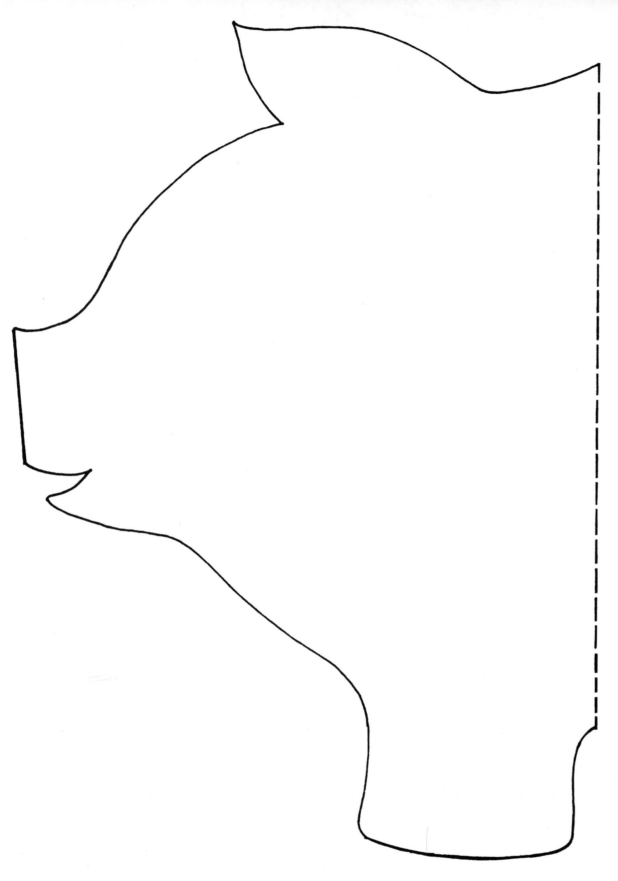

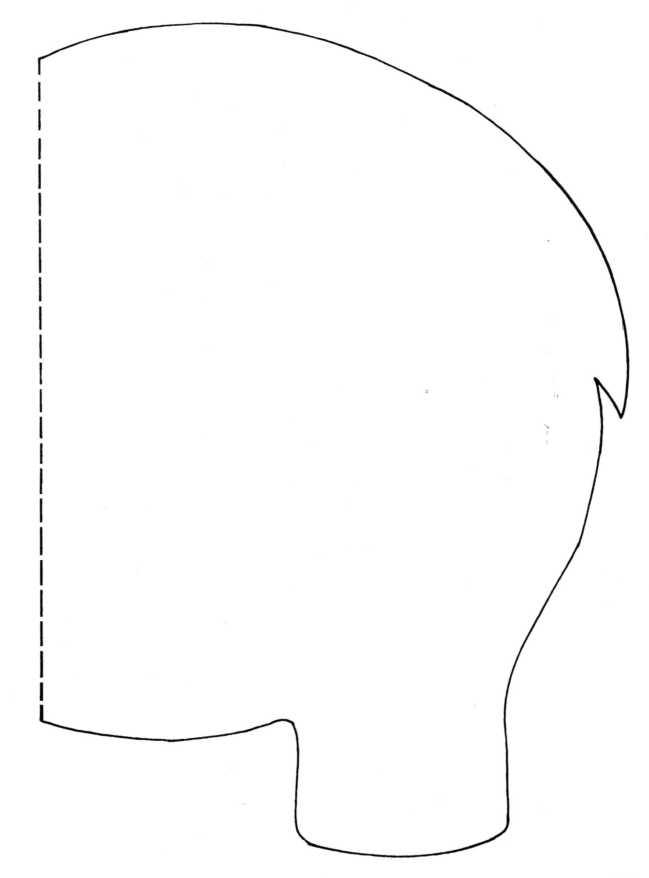

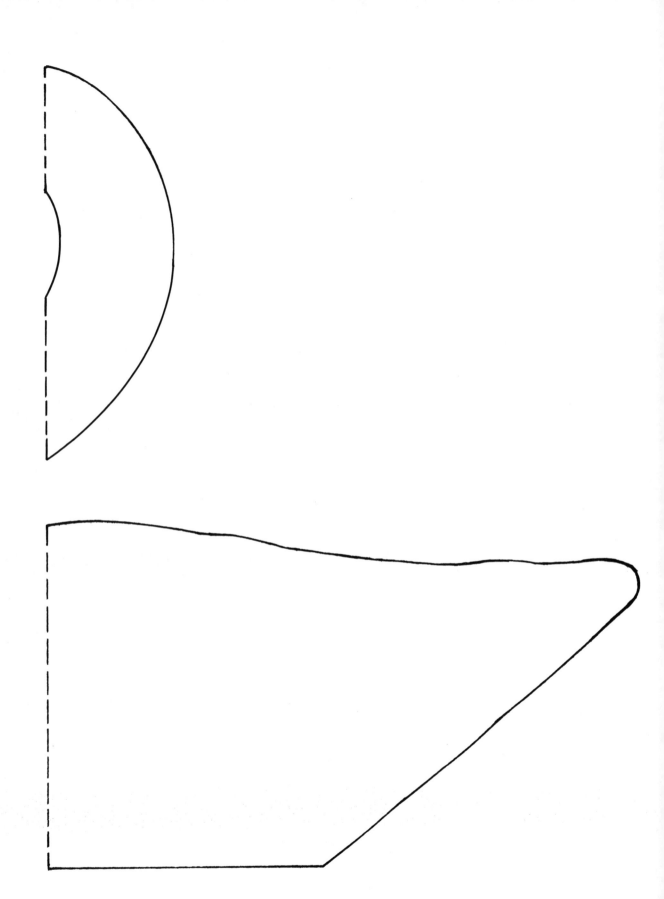

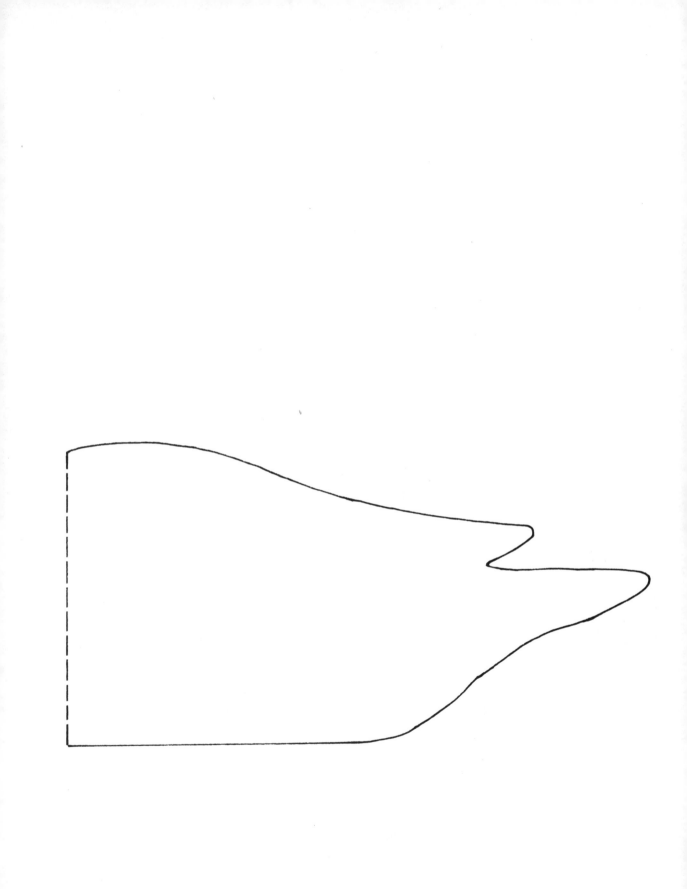

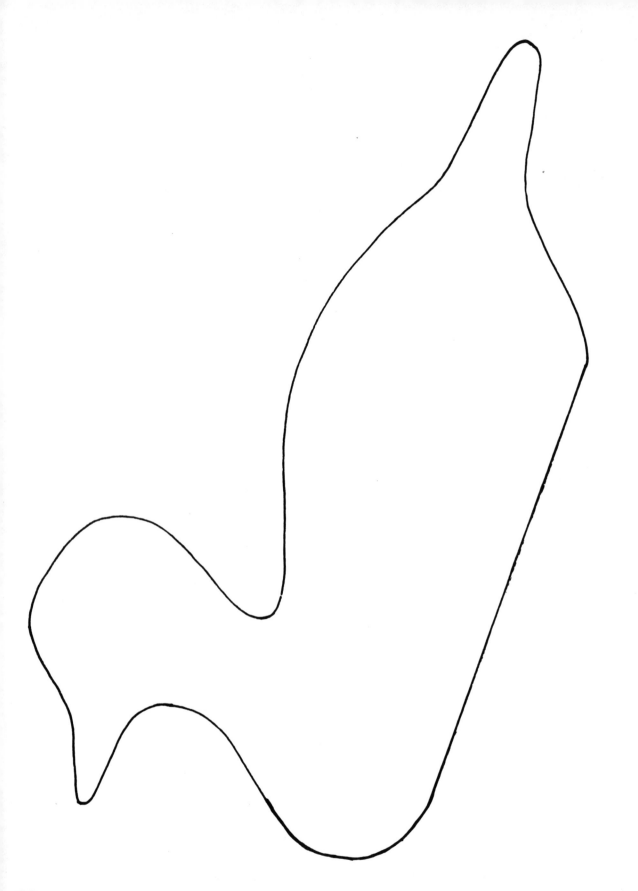

32

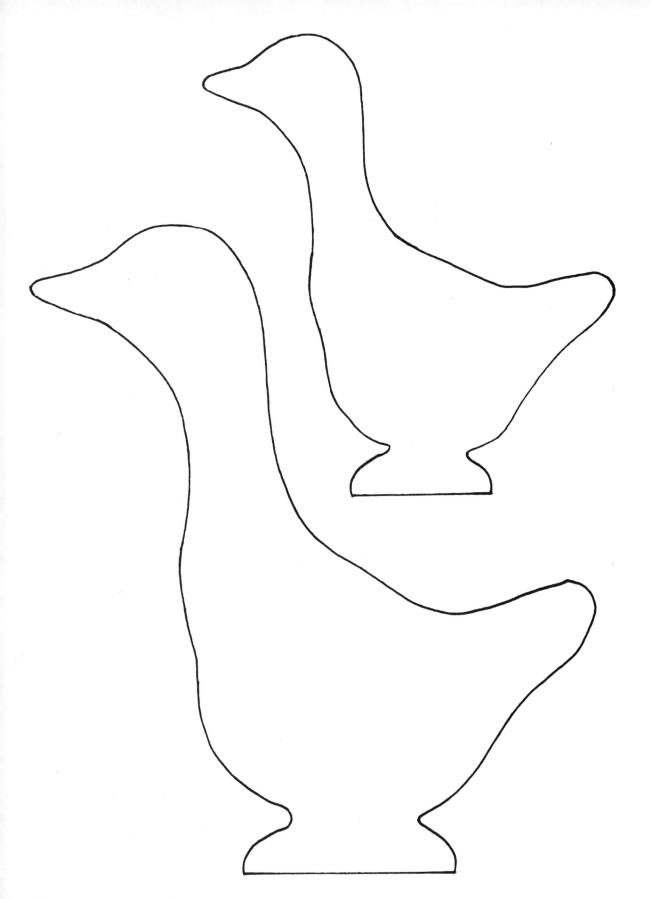

Geese.

Flowers/Leaves/Fruit

Tulips. Patterns can be found on the following page.

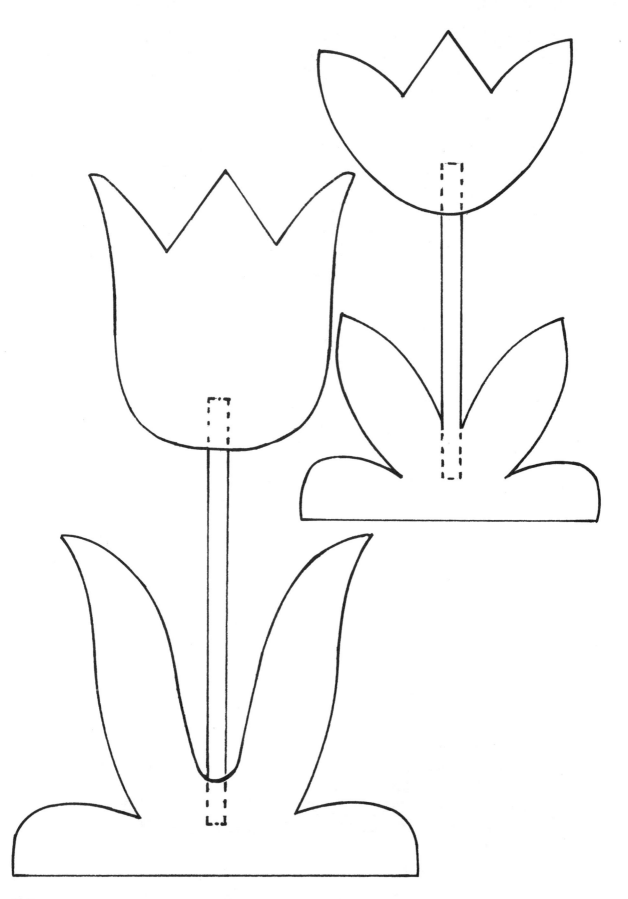

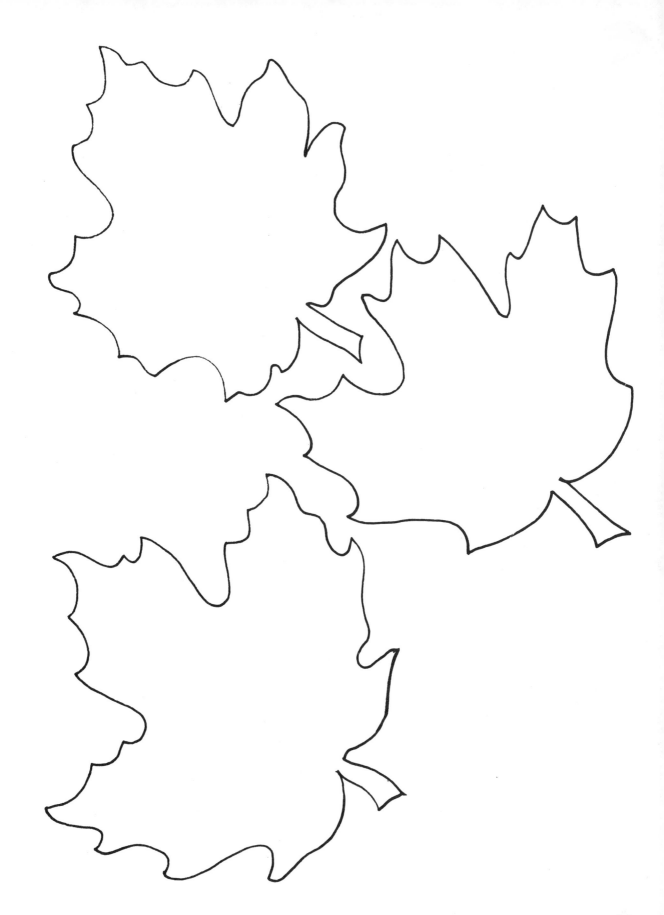

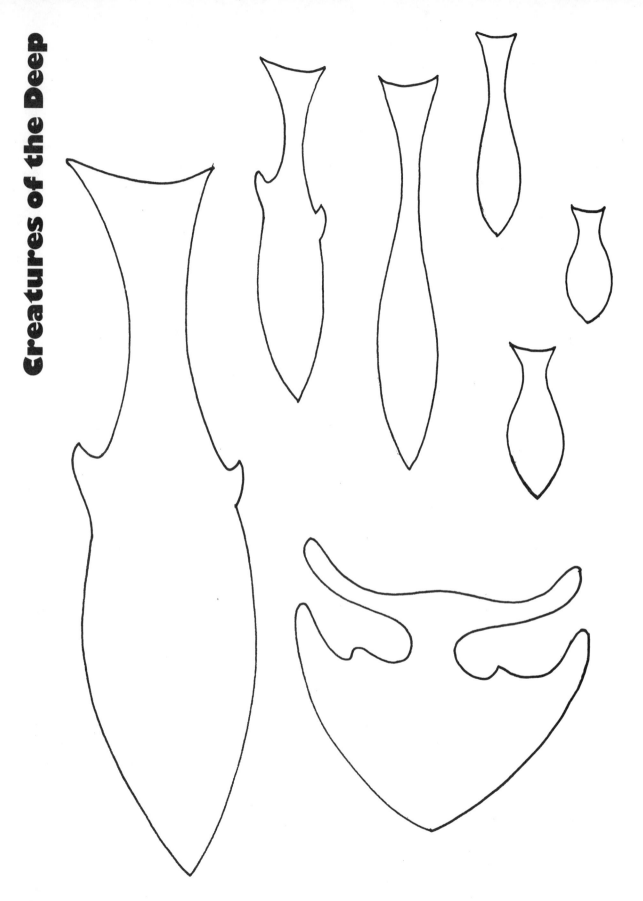

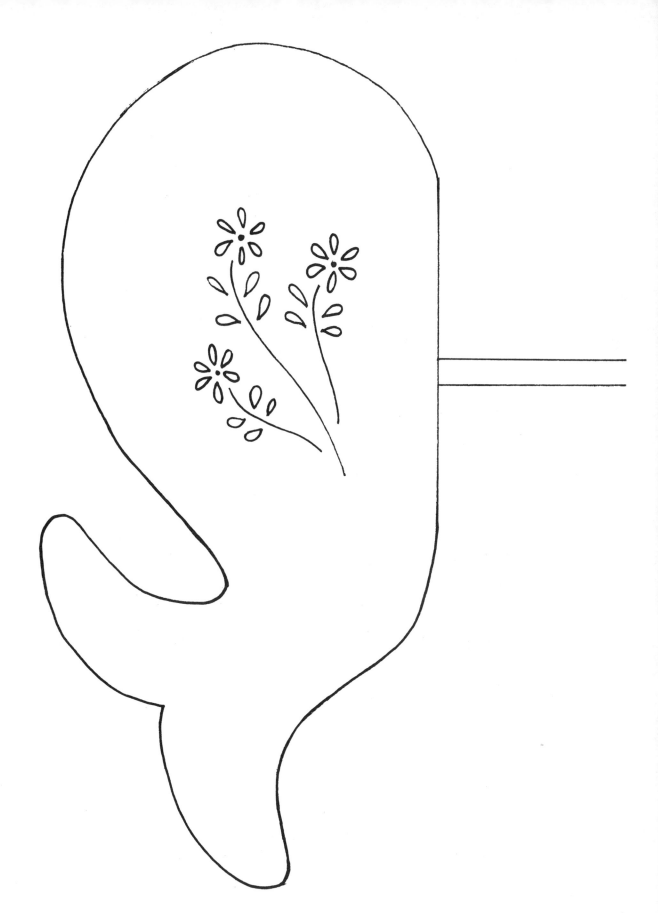

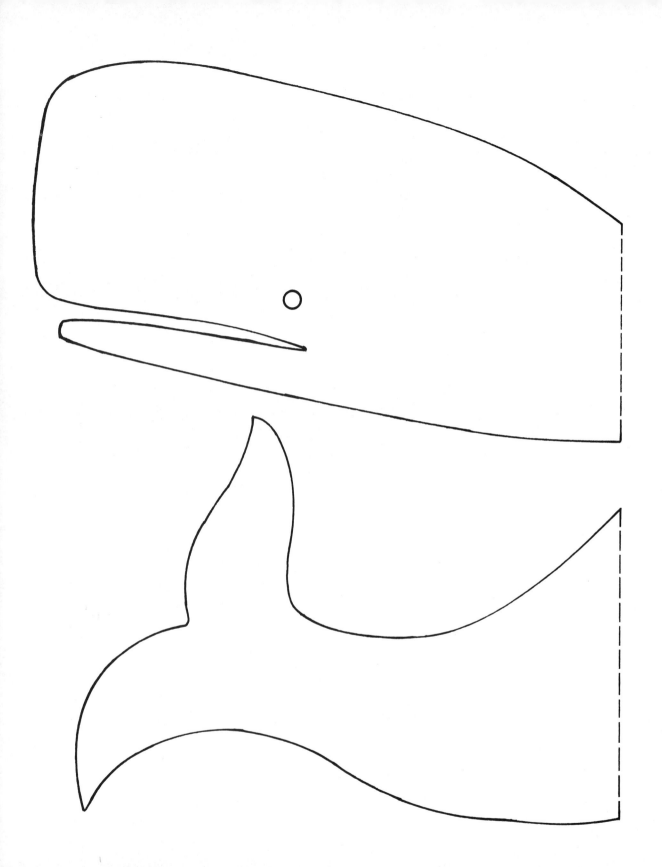

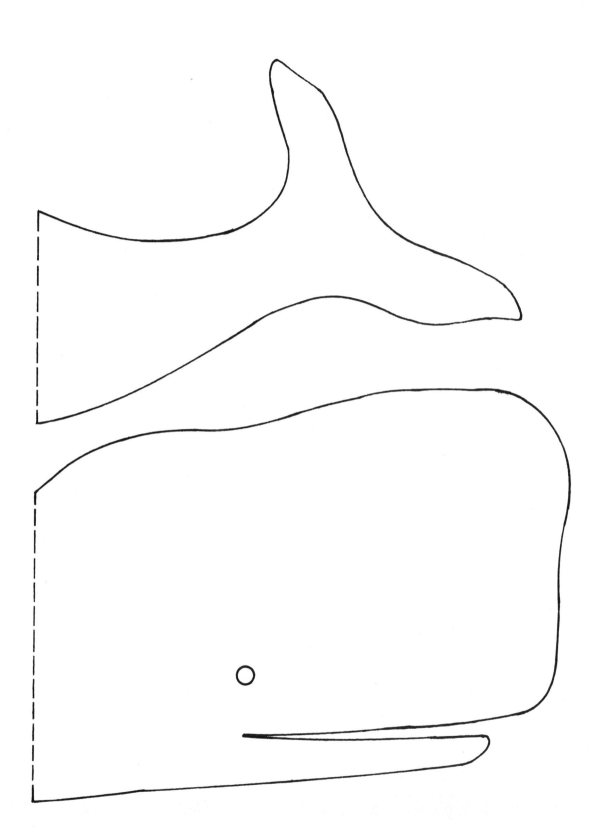

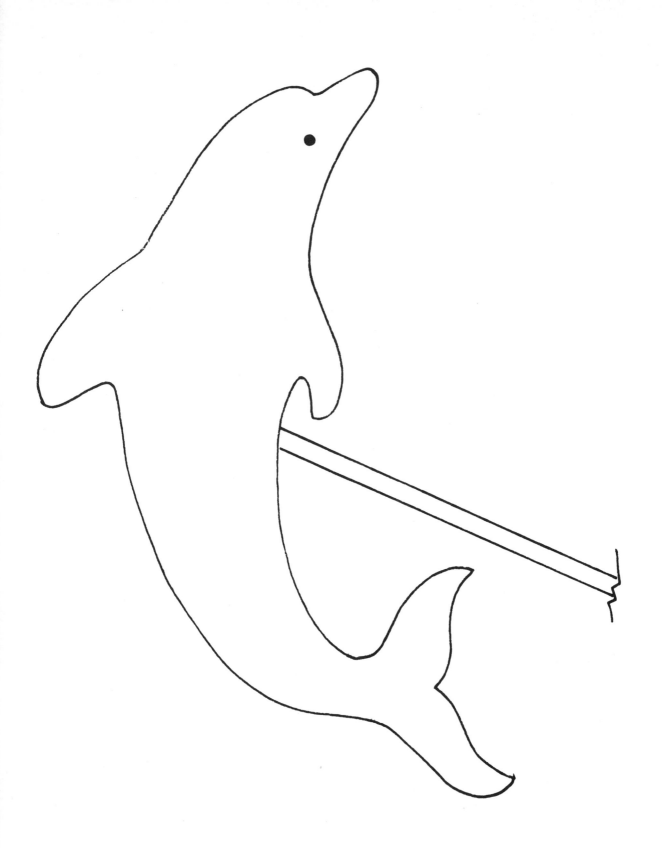

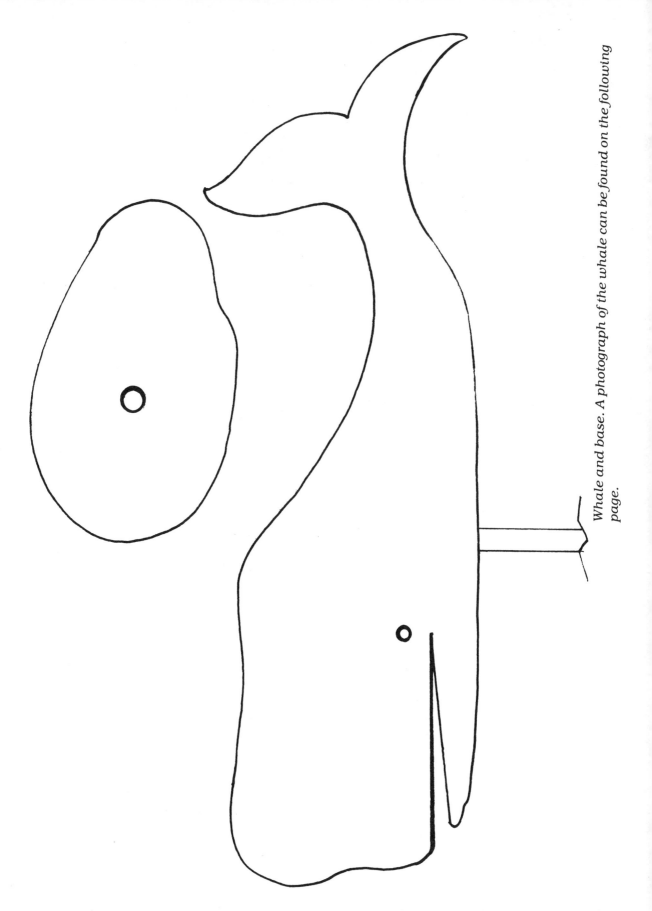

Whale and base. A photograph of the whale can be found on the following page.

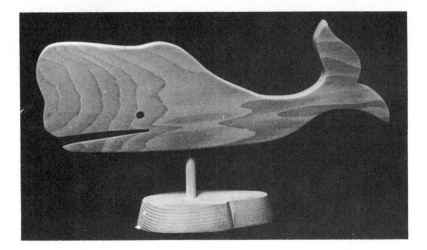

Birds

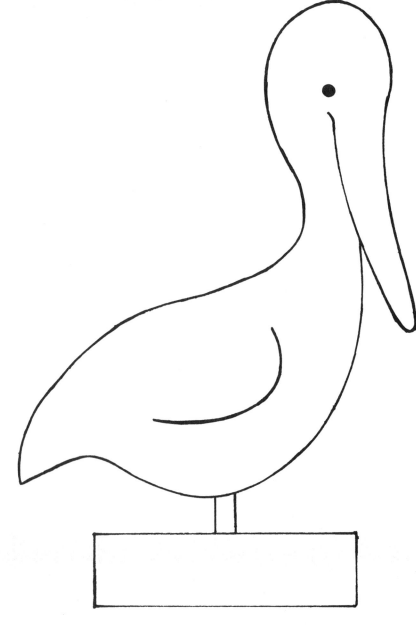

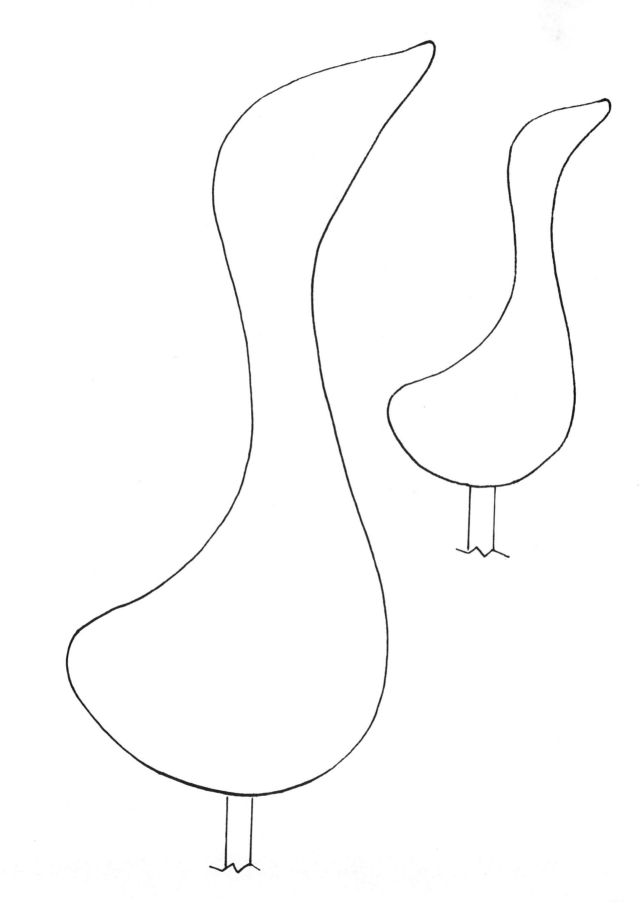

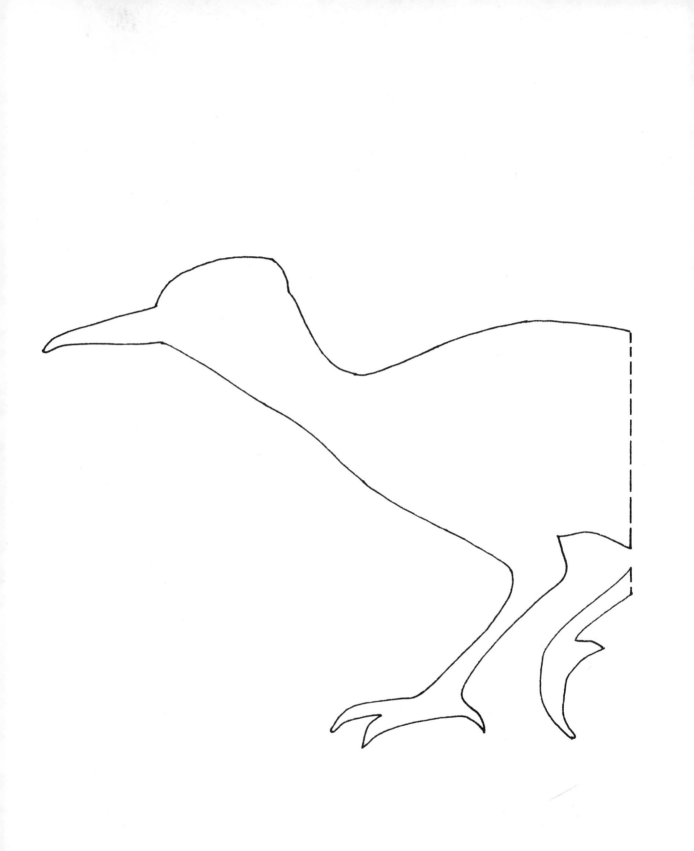

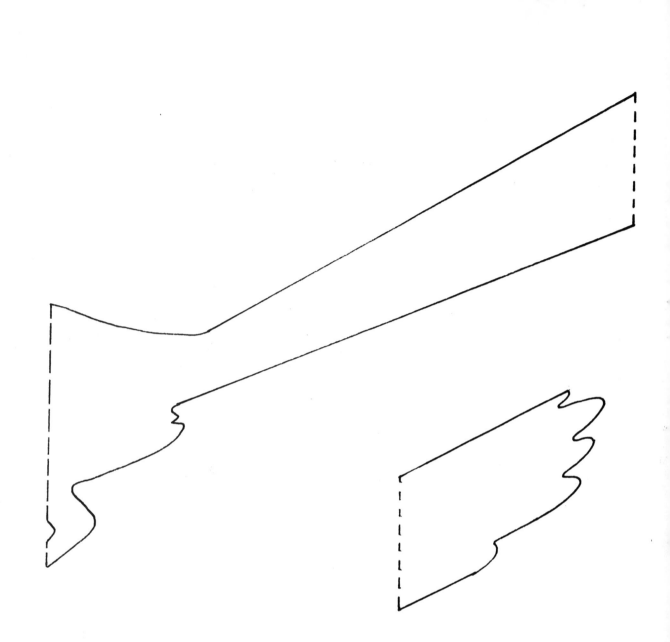

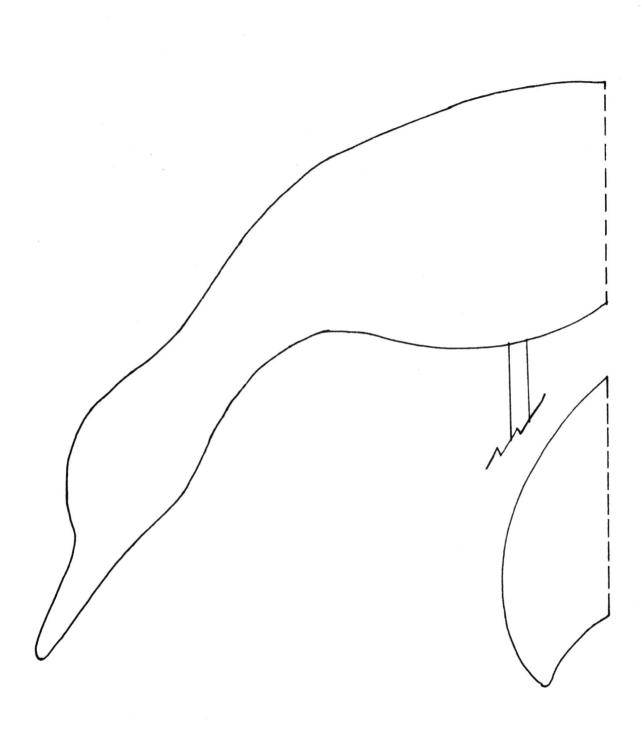

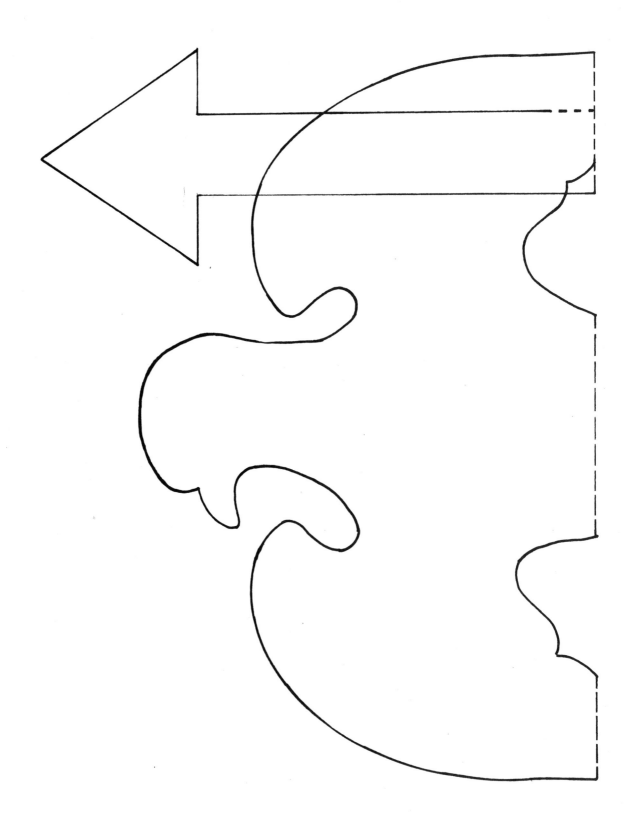

56

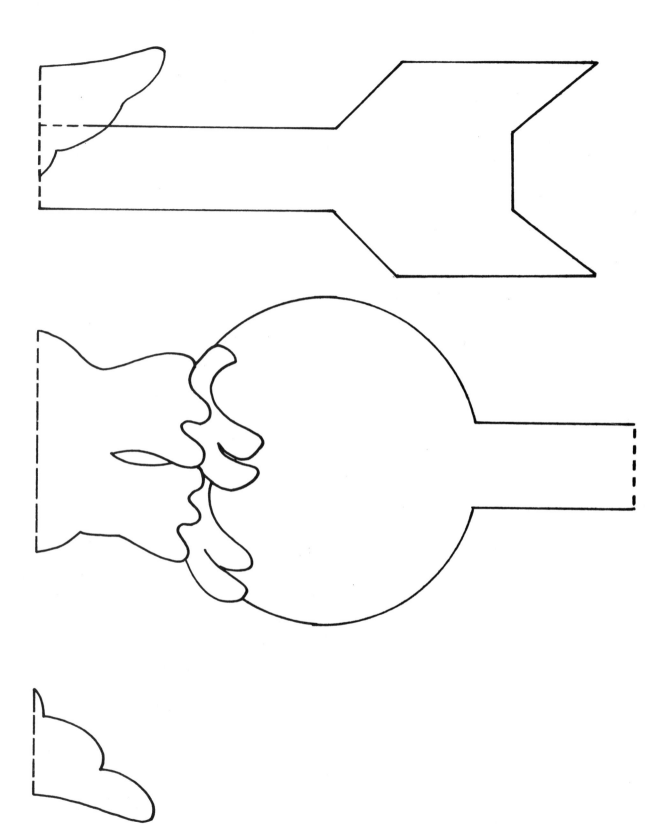

57

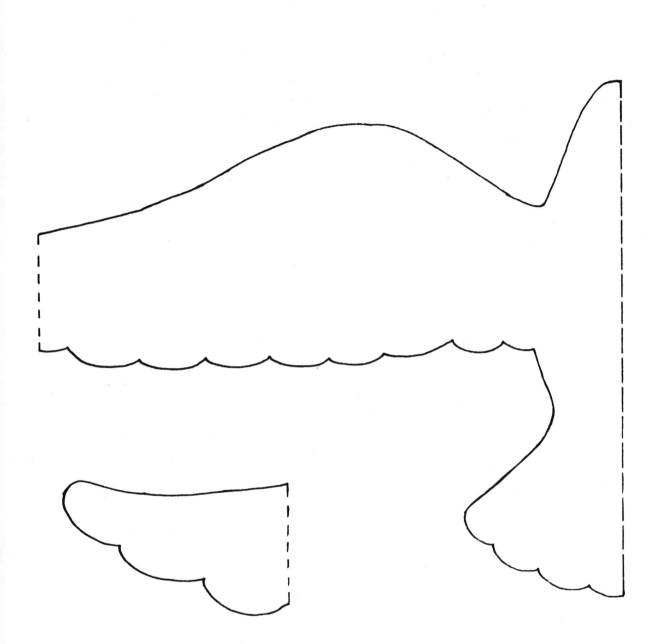

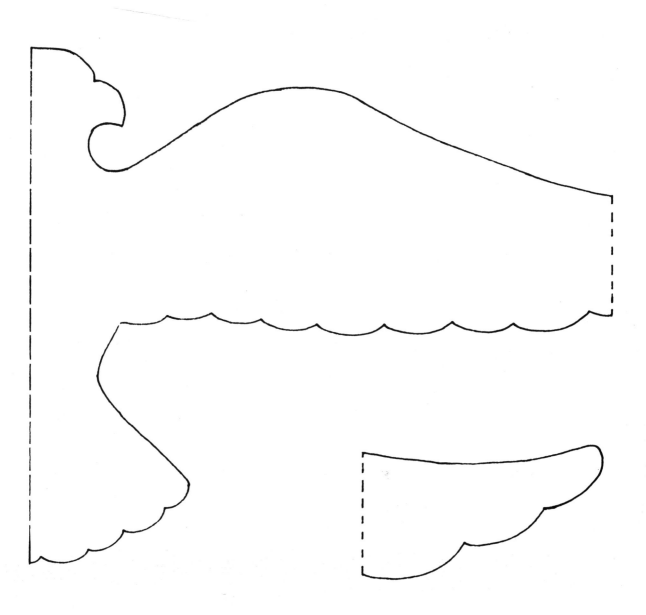

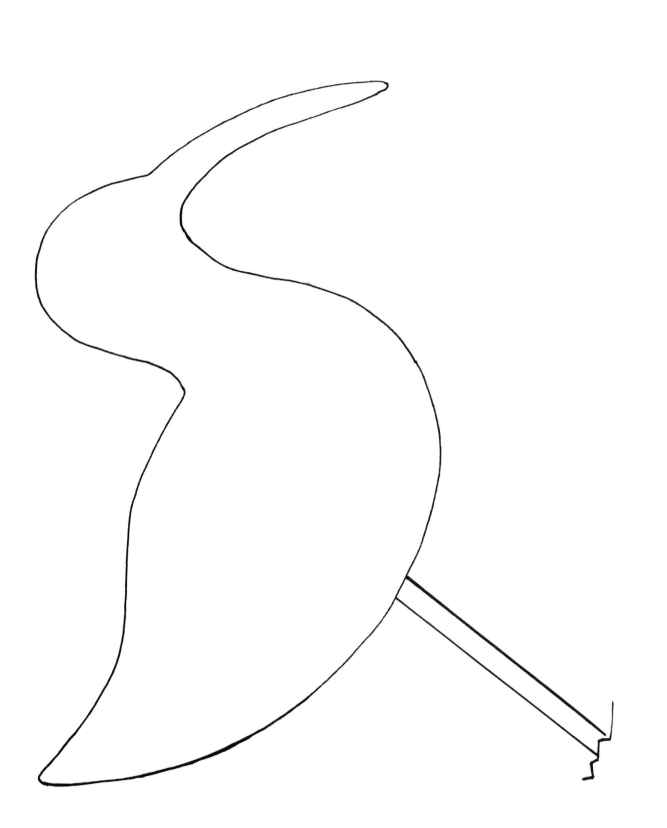

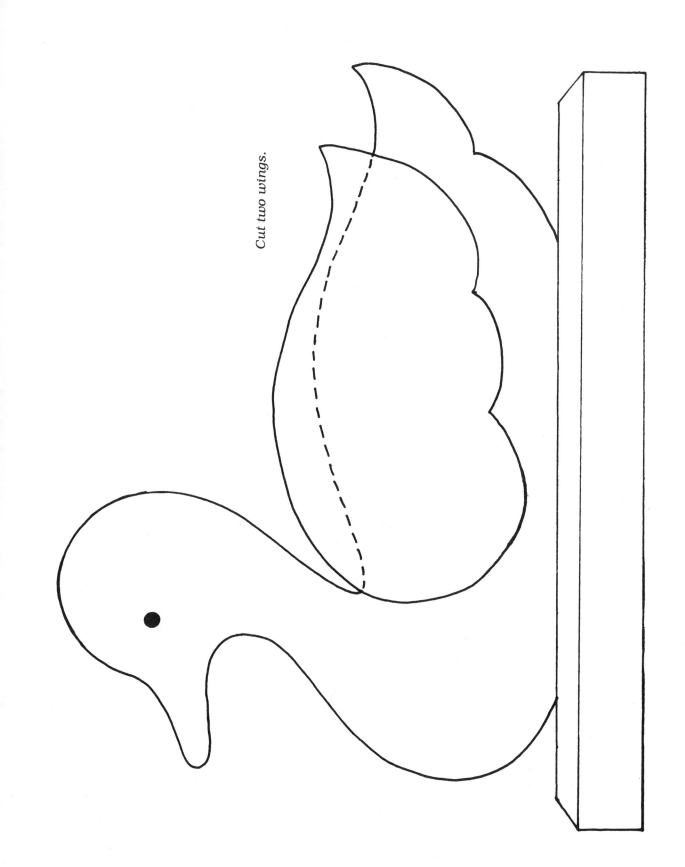

Cut two wings.

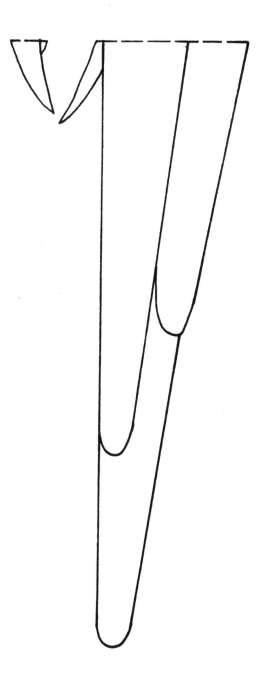

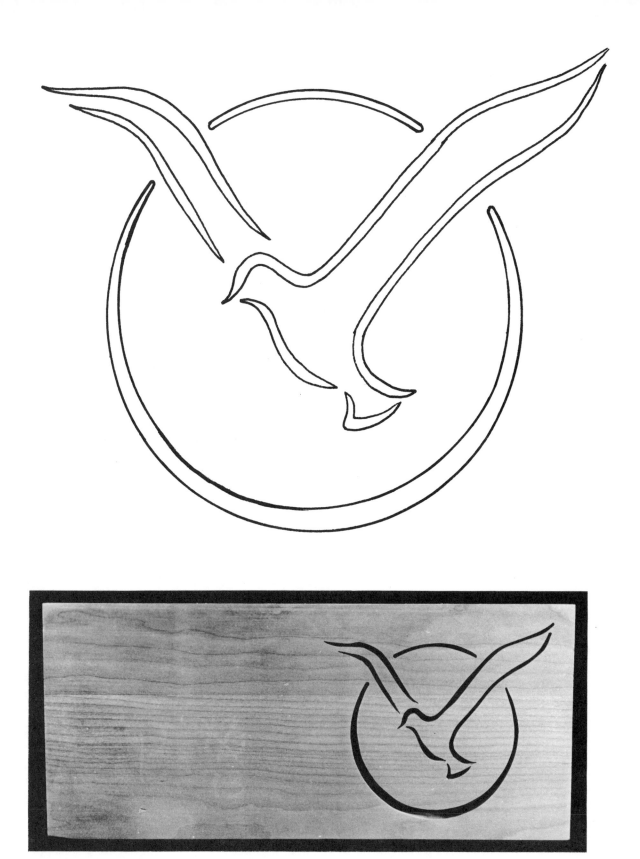

Gull design that has been cut through. Such designs can be used for sign-boards or clockfaces.

Key Racks

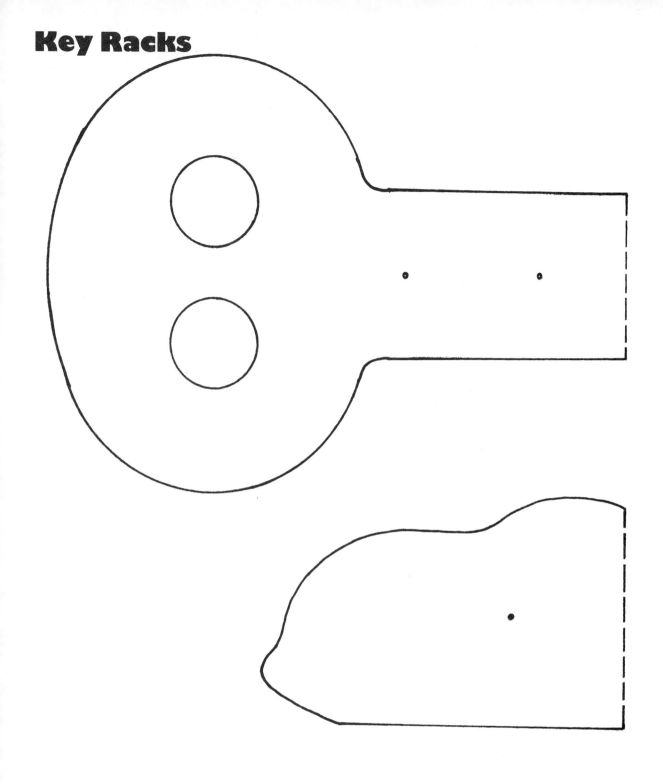

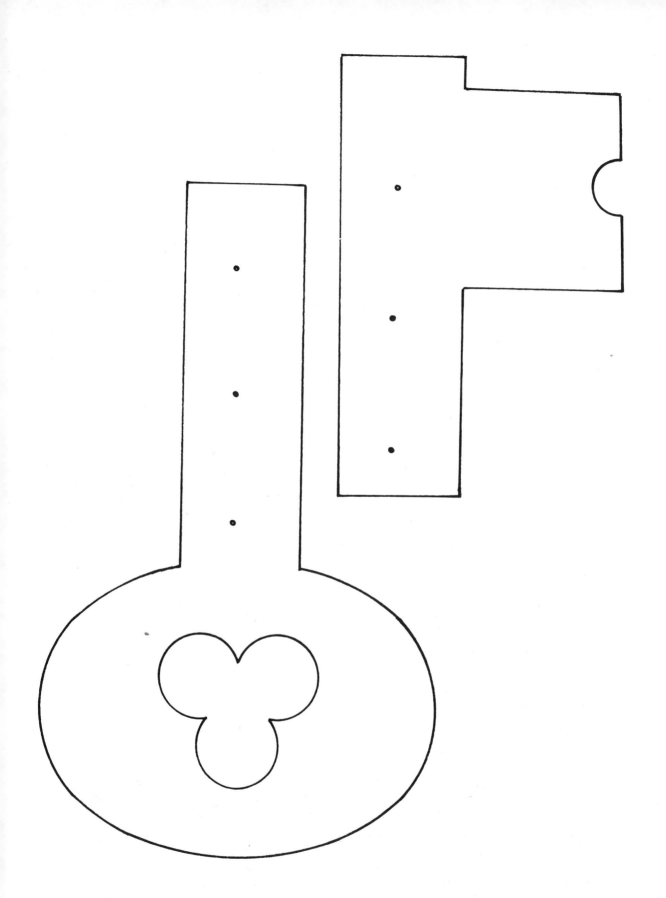

Interlocking Trees/Corner Shelves

Interlocking trees cut from ¼-inch plywood.

Corner shelf with ¼-inch-thick sides; the shelf is ⅜ inch thick.

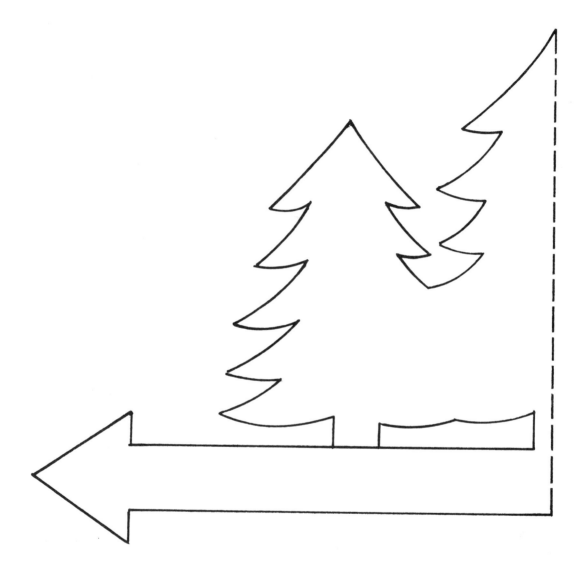

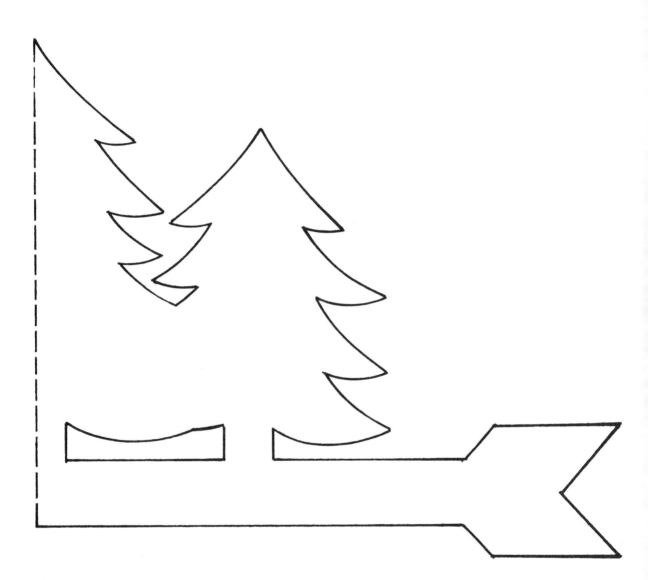

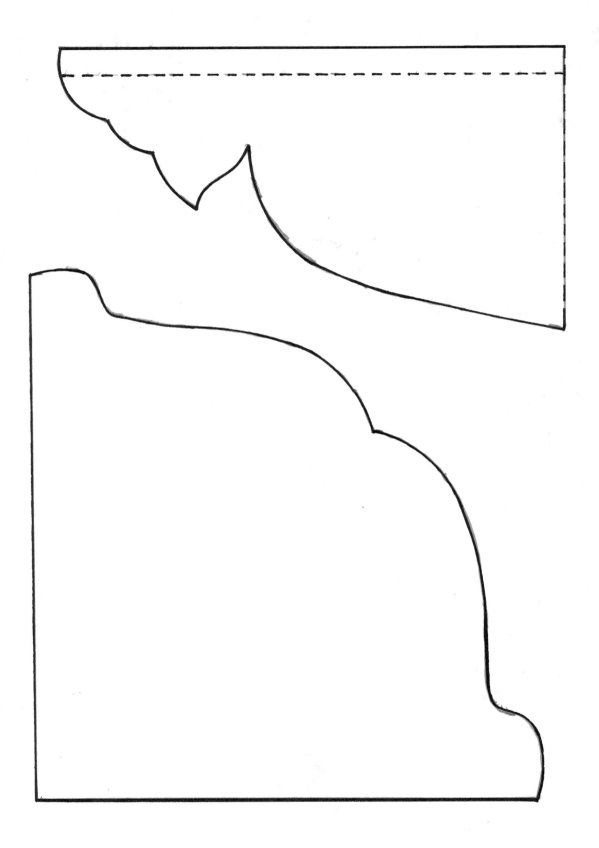

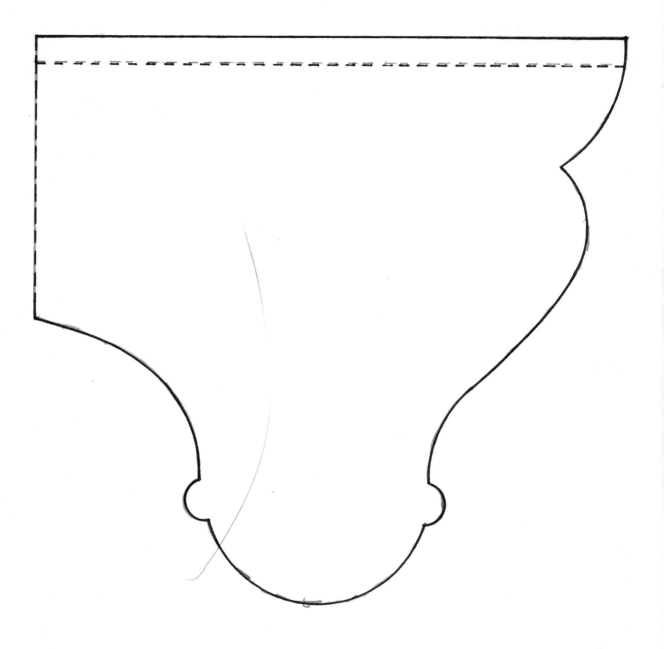

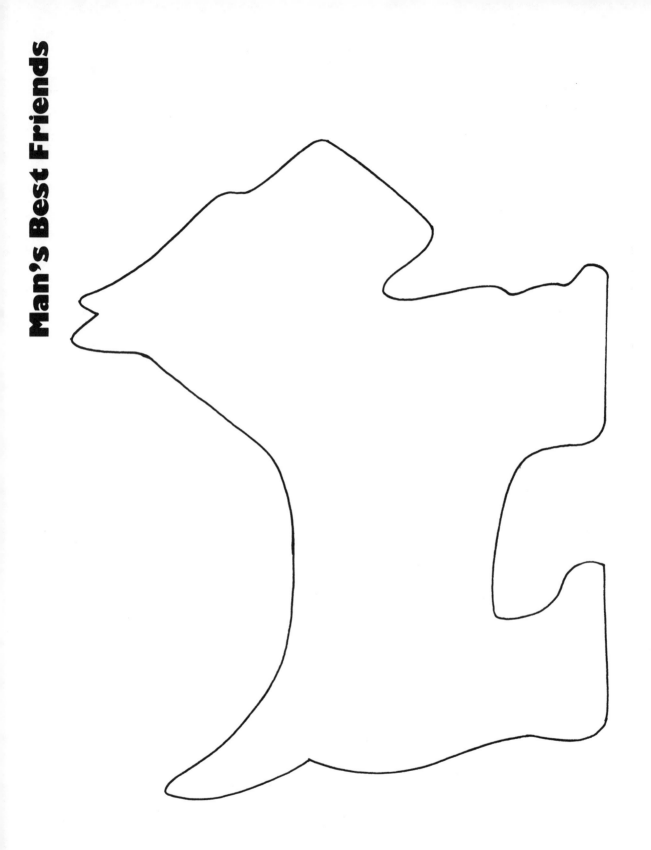

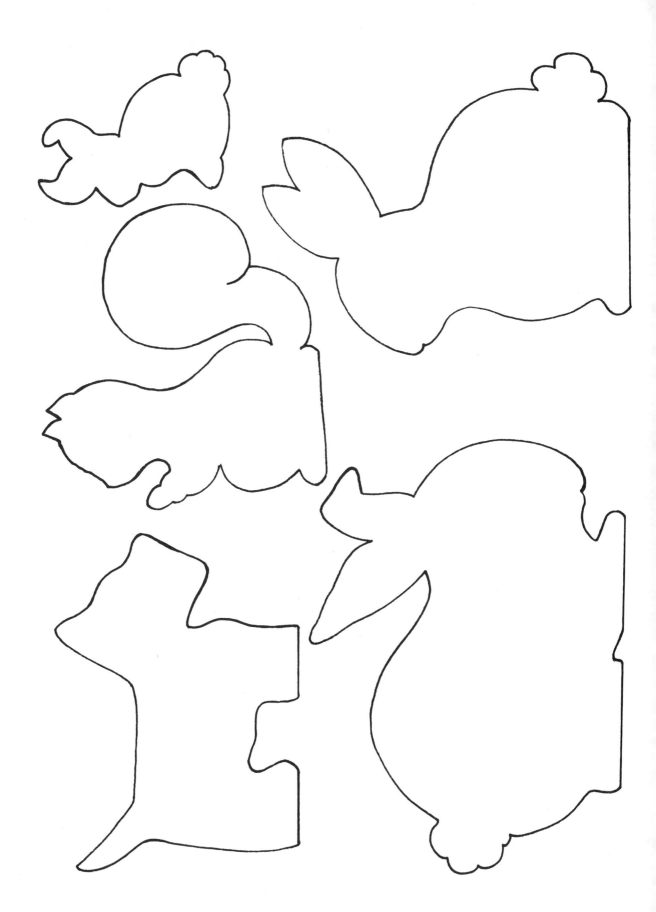

Goldilocks and the Three Bears.

Mini-Animal Cutouts

Mini-animal cutouts.

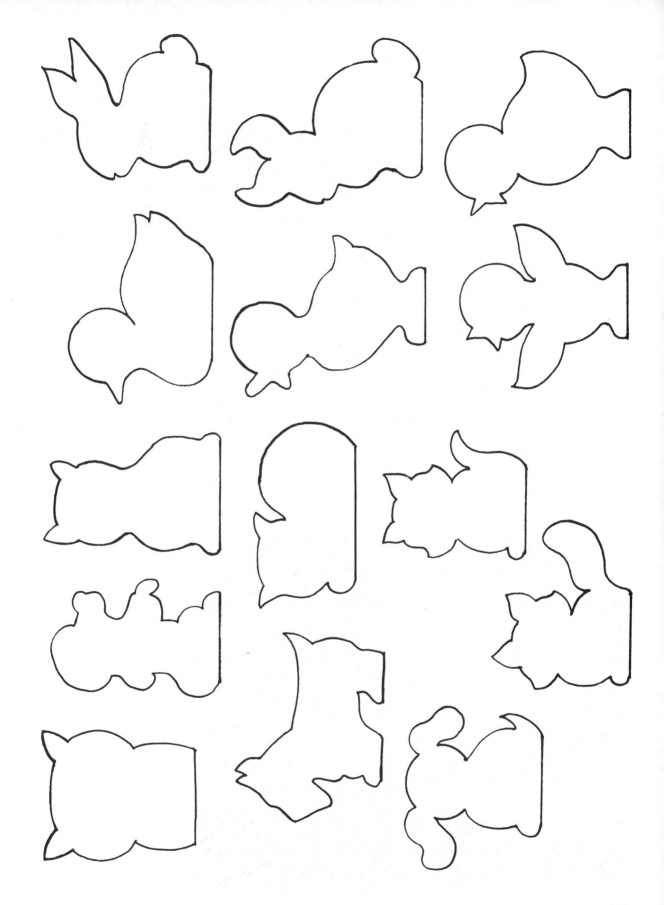

Belt Hook Designs

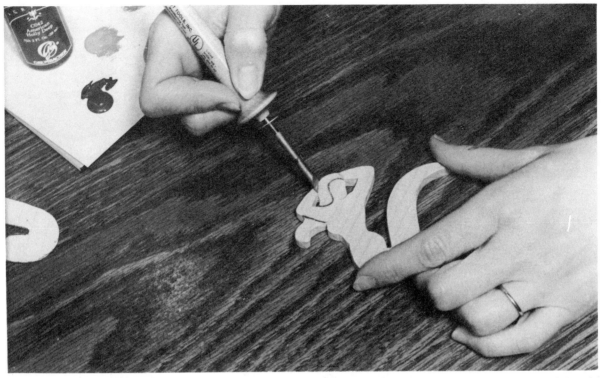

Woodburning lines on a mermaid belt hook.

A variety of belt hook designs cut from ¼- to ⅜-inch stock.

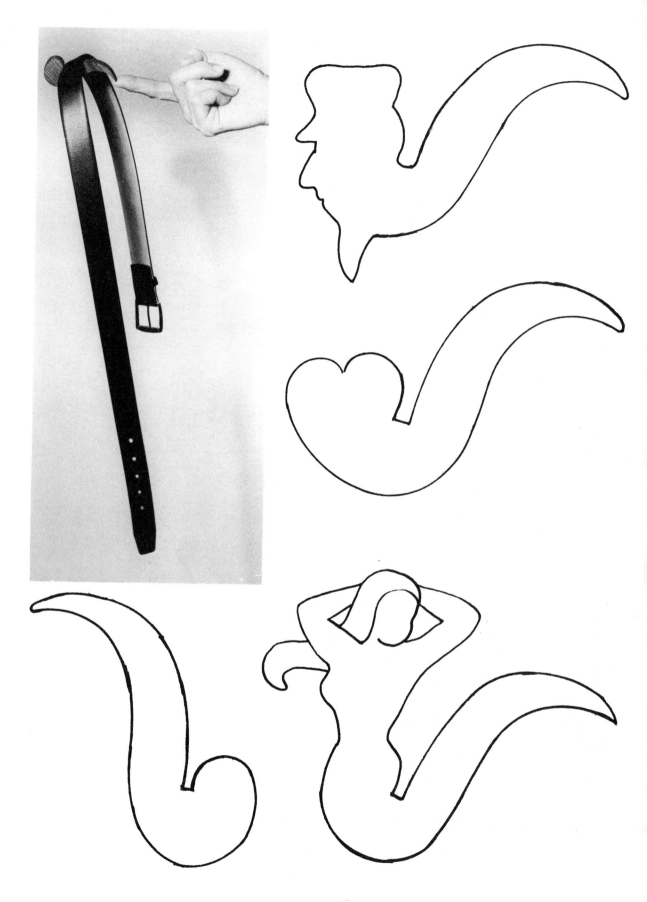

Cat and Flowers

Cat and patterns. Patterns for these flowers can be found on pages 36 and 37.

Dimensional Animal Cutouts

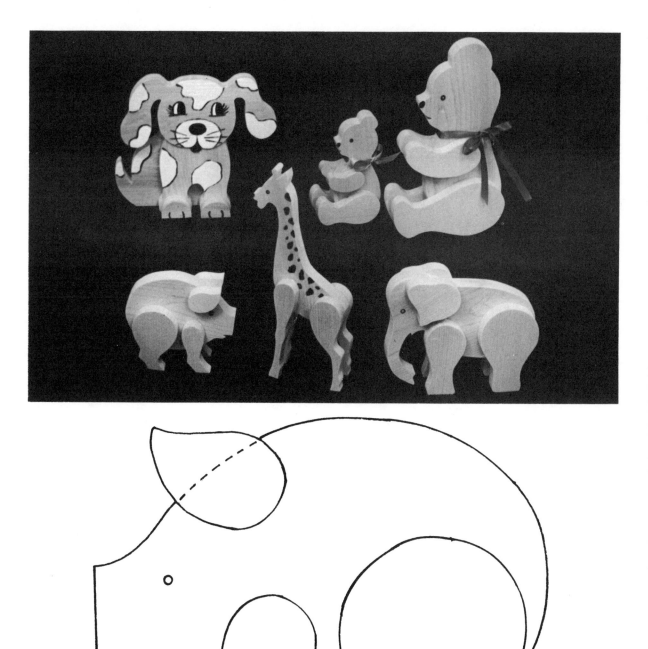

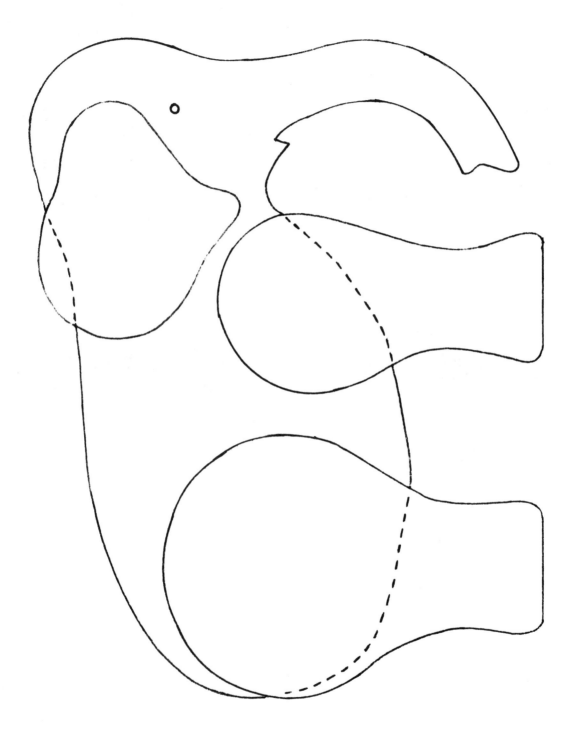

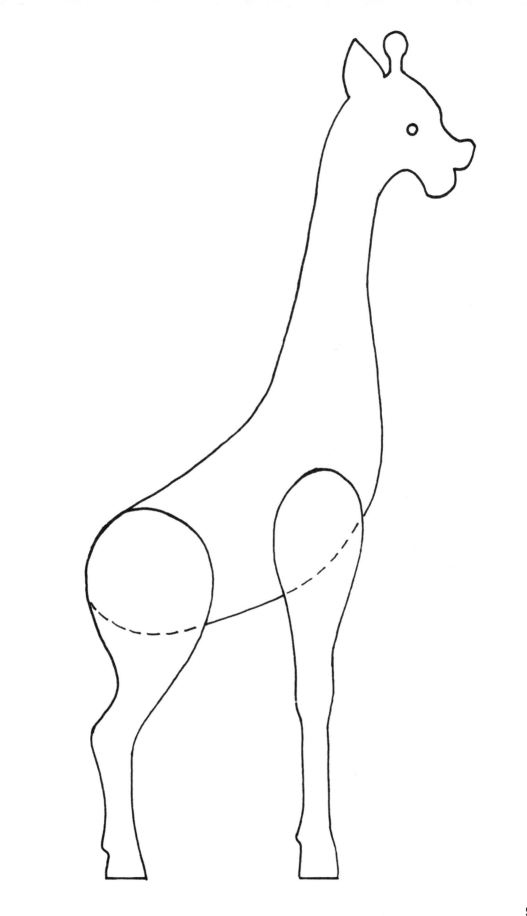

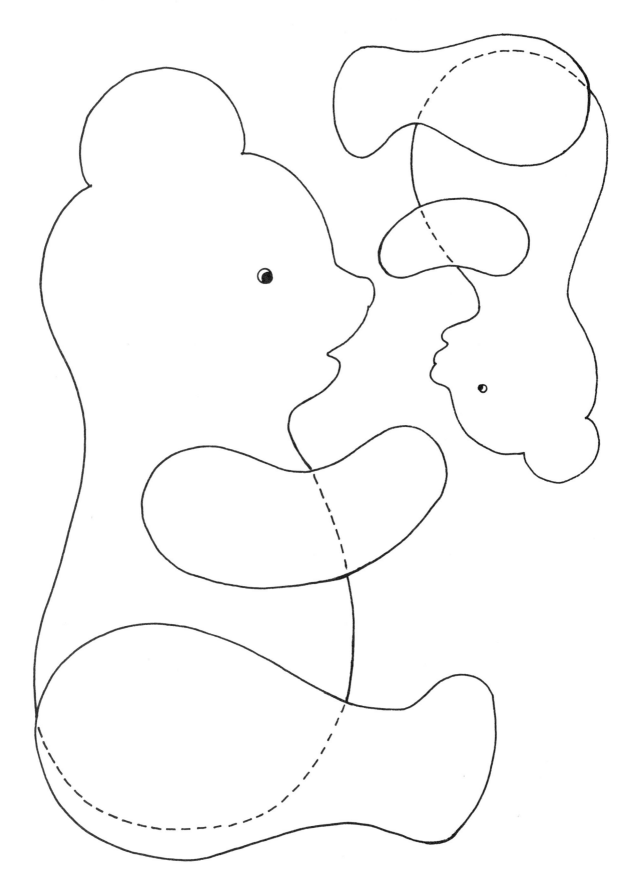

Refrigerator Magnets/ "Pets on a Stick"

The refrigerator magnets are cut from ¼-inch stock; epoxy is put on purchased magnets. Patterns for refrigerator magnets can be found on pages 99 and 100.

"Pets on a stick." Patterns for the "Pets" can be found on pages 101 and 102.

More Friendly Creatures

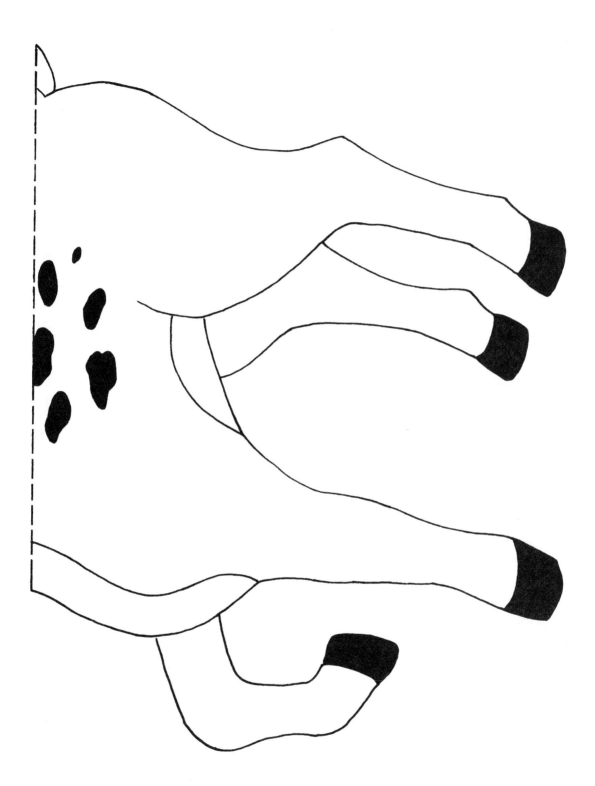

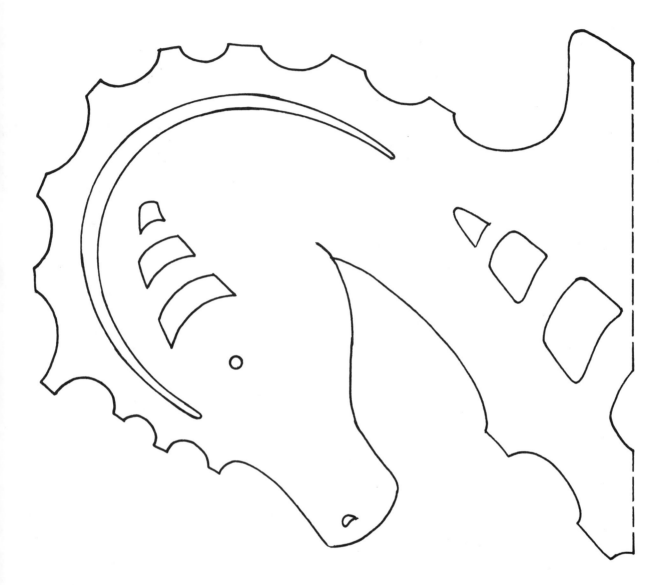

Napkin Rings/Puzzles

Napkin rings. Patterns can be found on pages 109–111.

Puzzles. Above: Cutout from thick stock. Below: Inlay puzzle cut from ¼-inch plywood with ¼-inch plywood backing. Patterns can be found on pages 112–135.

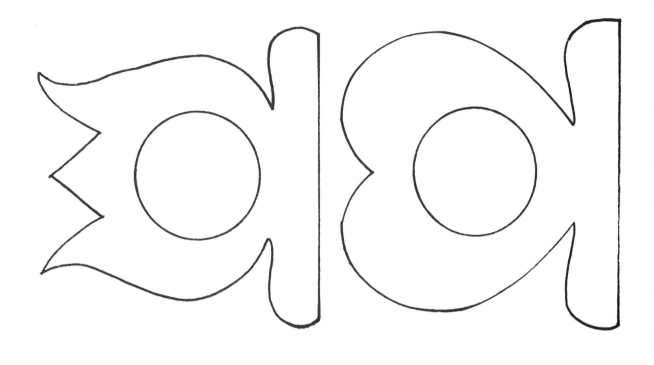

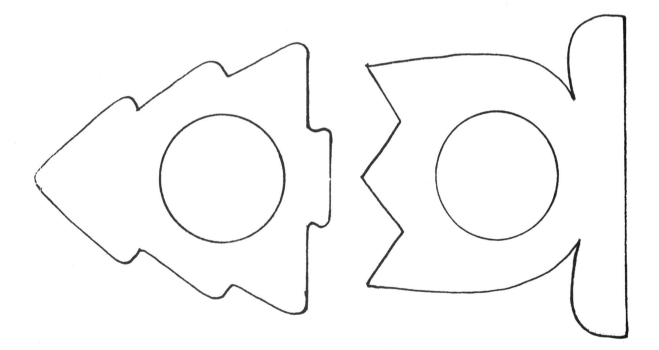

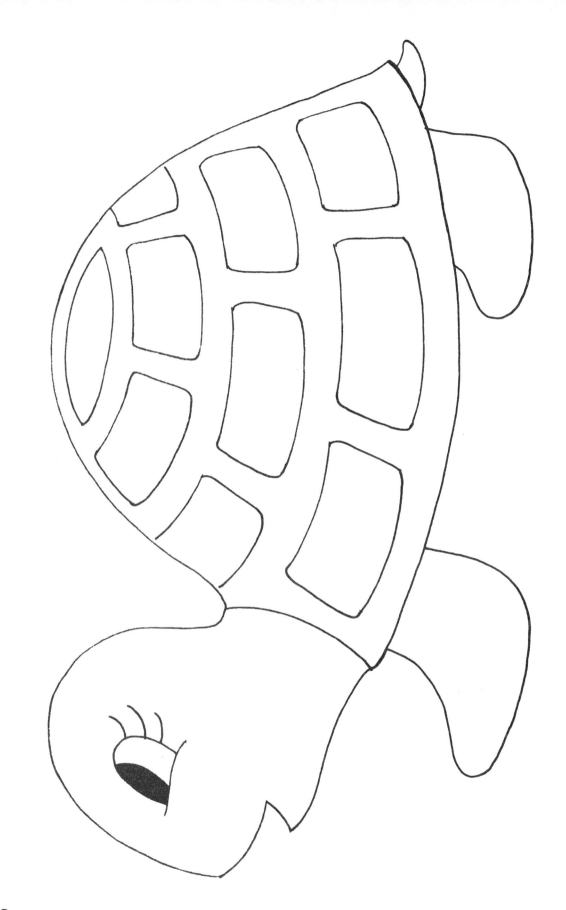

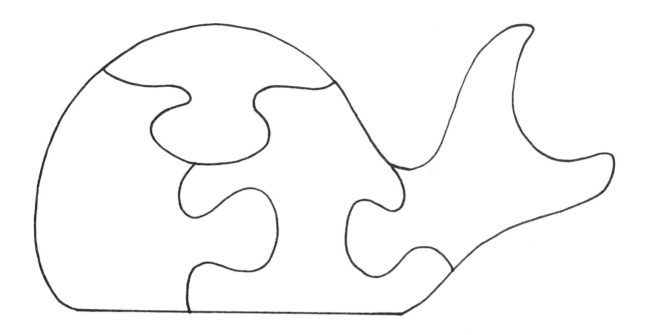

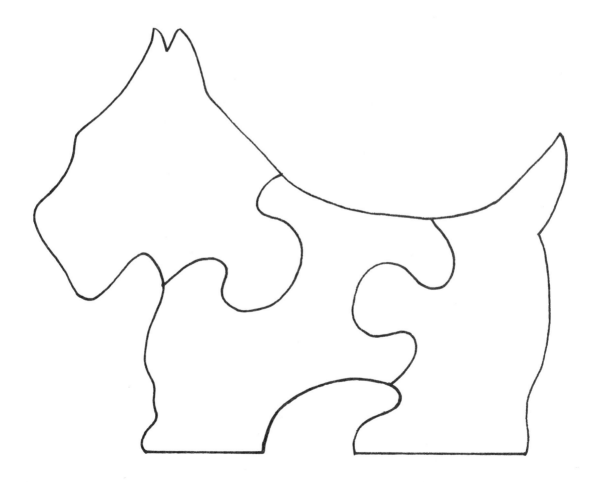

127

130

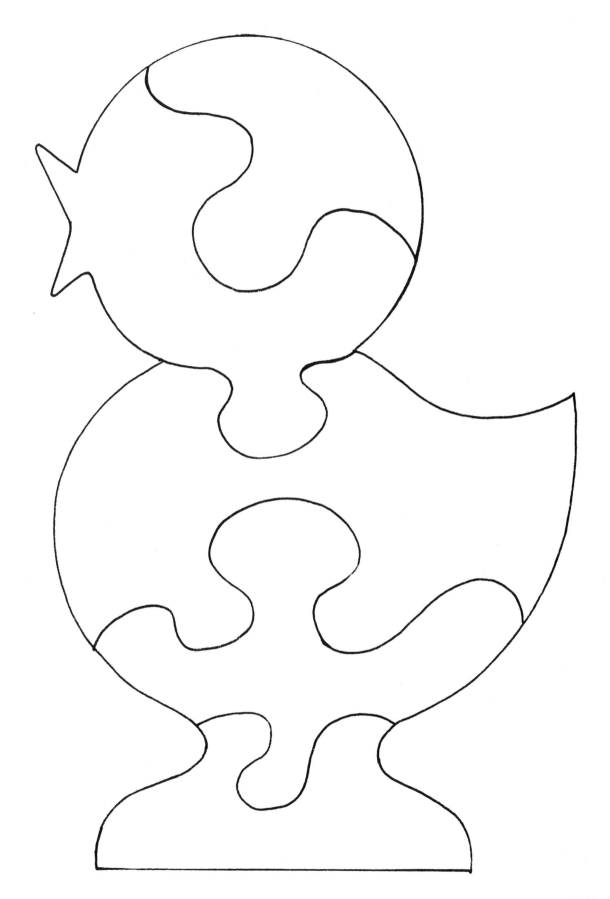

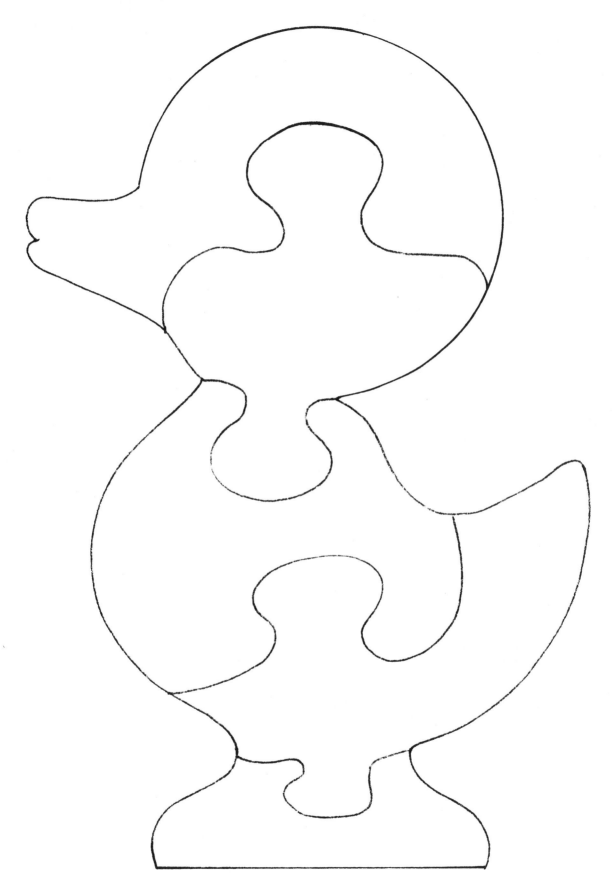

135

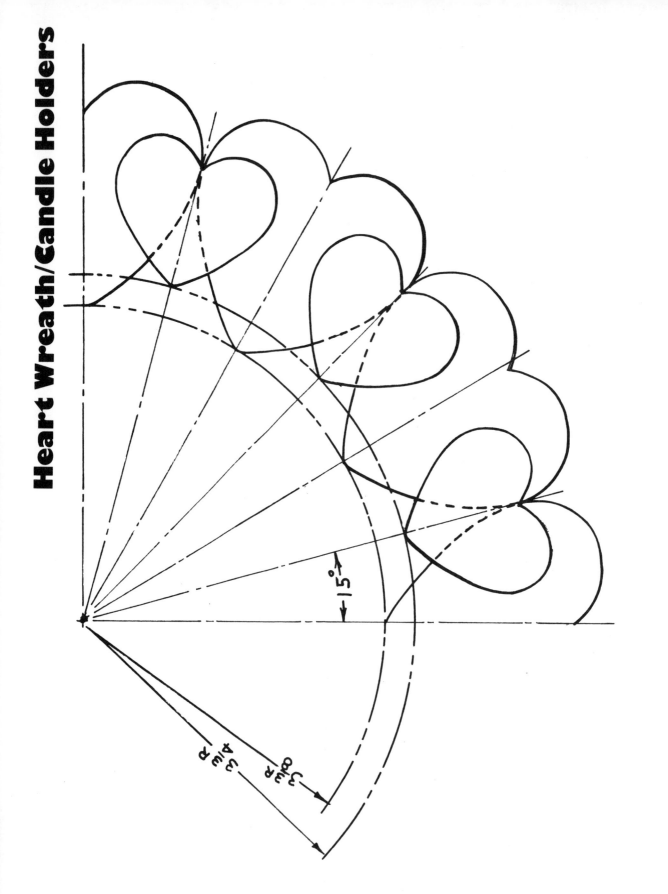

15°

3R

3 3/4 R

3 8/9

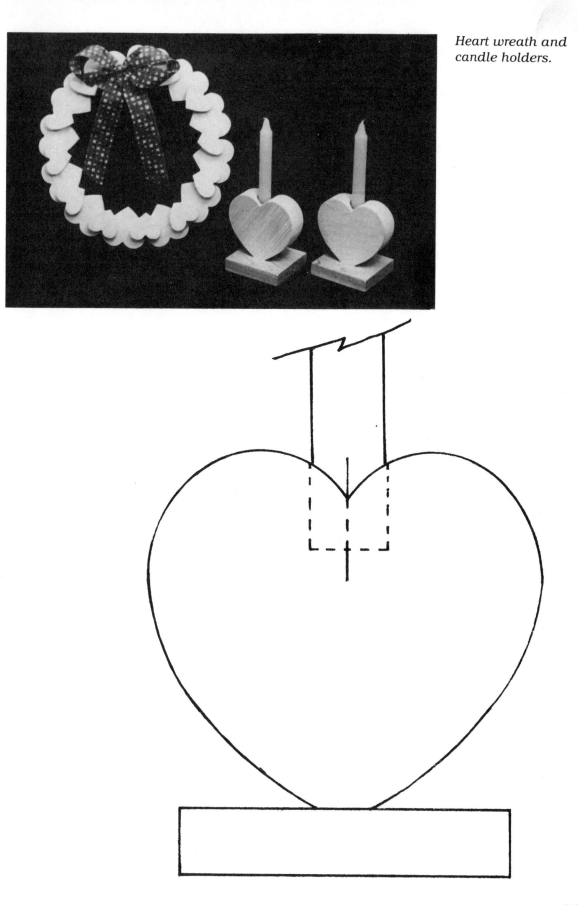

Heart wreath and candle holders.

Jewelry/Ornaments

These items of jewelry were made from brass and ⅛-inch-thick exotic hardwoods. The key chains were made from ¼-inch plywood.

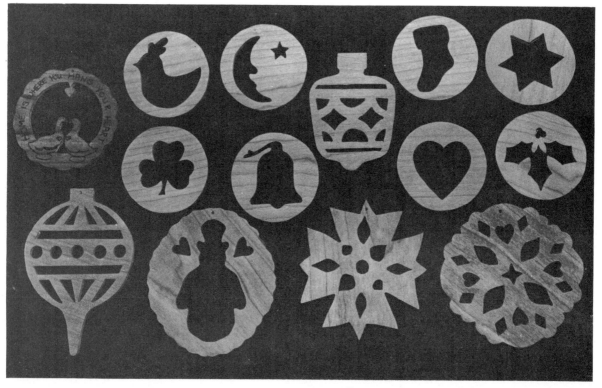

Ornaments made from ¼-inch material.

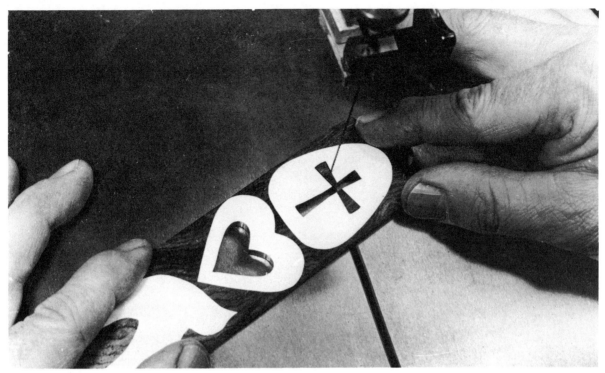

Sawing out jewelry. Paper patterns are glued to the work with rubber cement.

Use epoxy to bond findings to the cutouts.

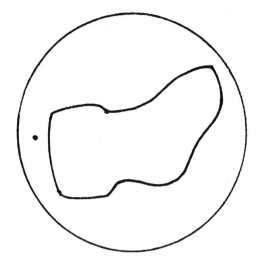

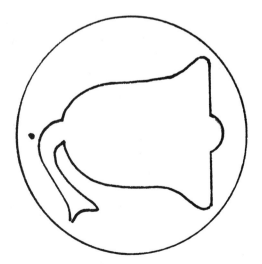

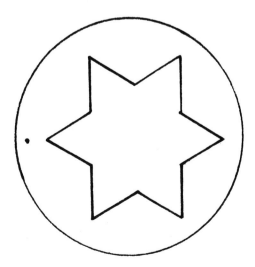

Candle Holders/Pegboards/Brackets

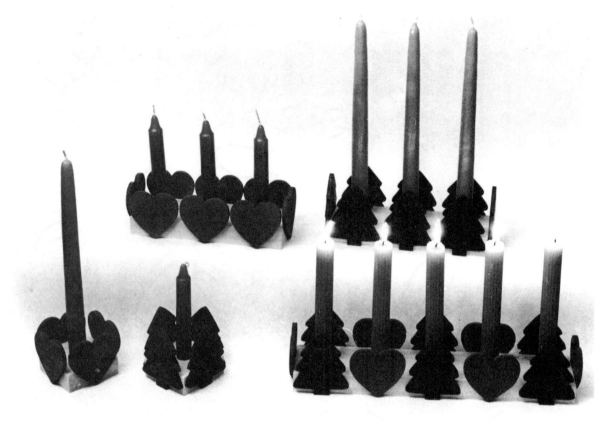

Candle holders. Use ¼-inch material for cutouts. Patterns can be found on pages 152 and 153.

Pegboards.

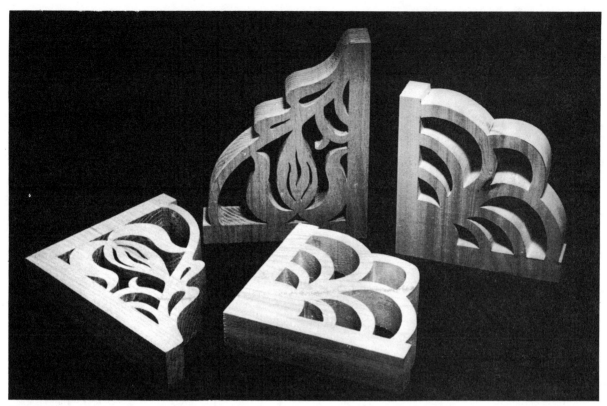

Brackets.

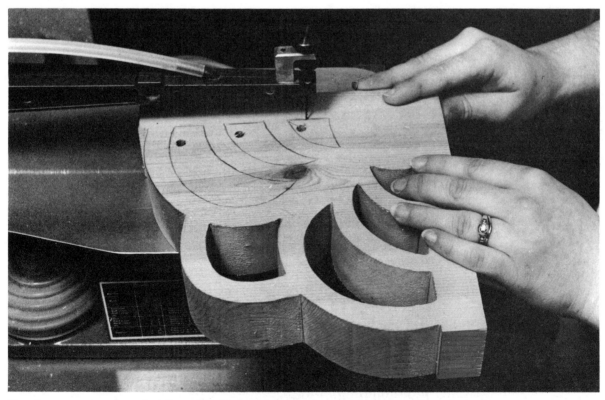

Sawing a corner bracket from 1¾-inch-thick stock.

151

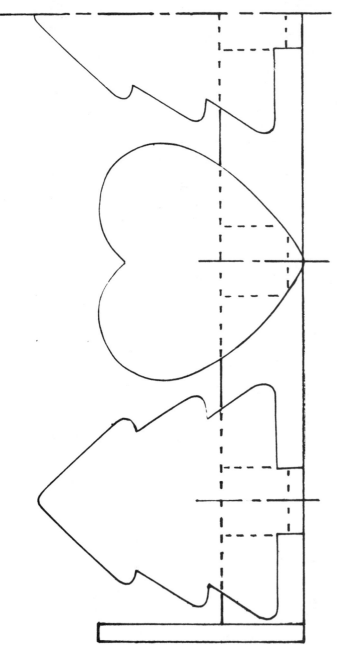

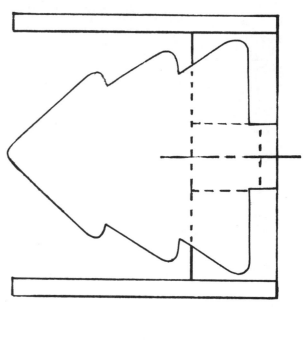

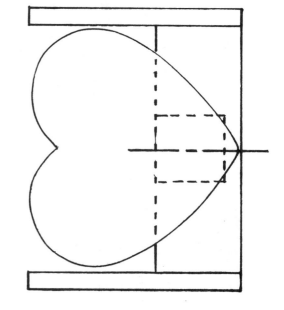

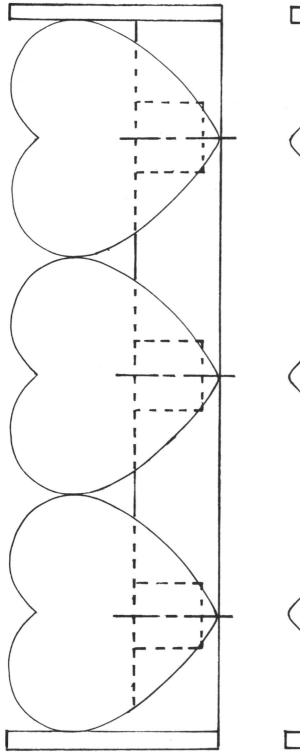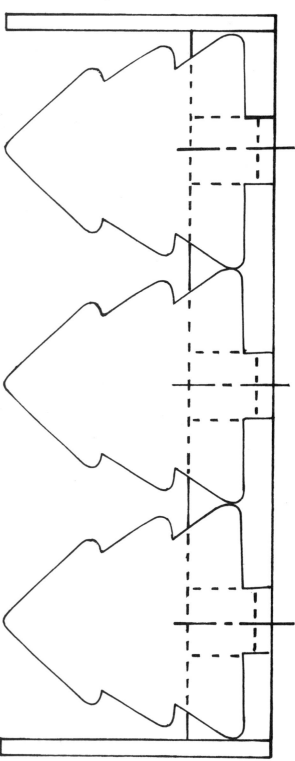

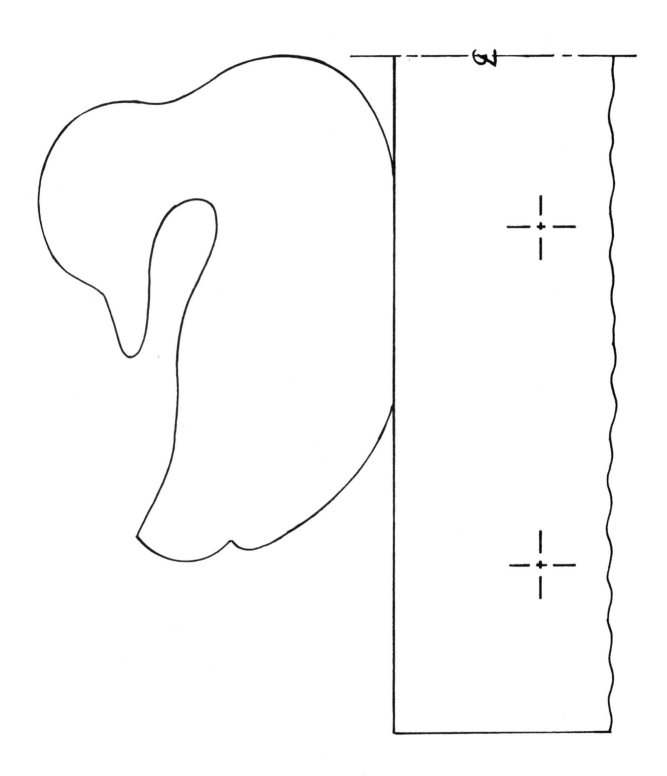

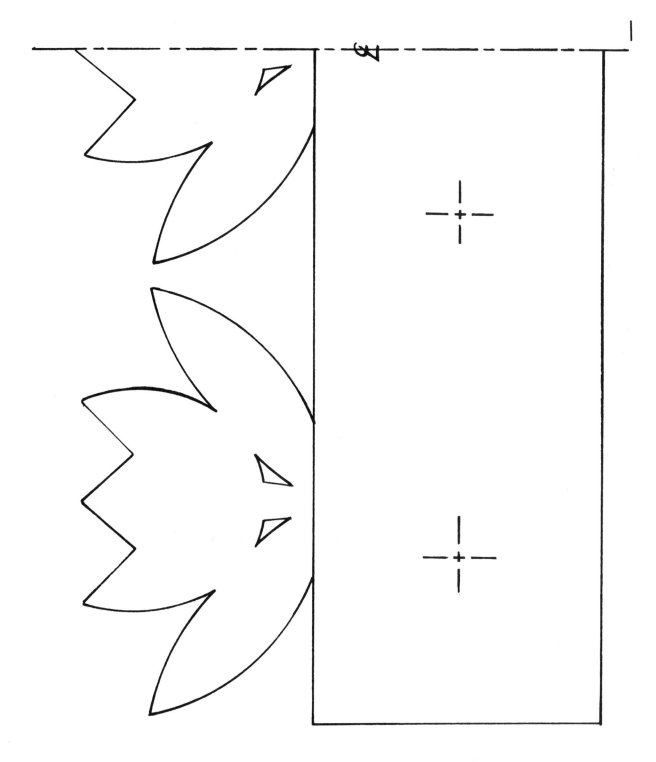

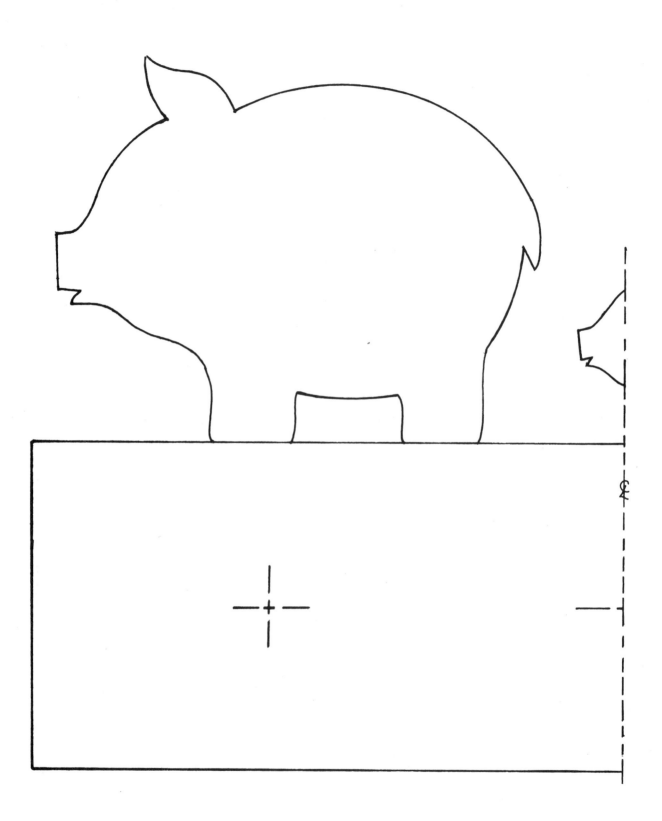

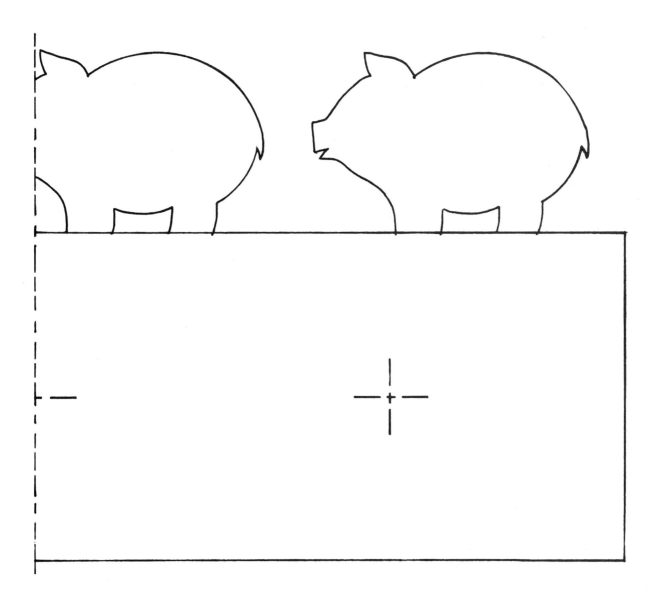

A

ALIGN A's

A

ALIGN A's.

162

164

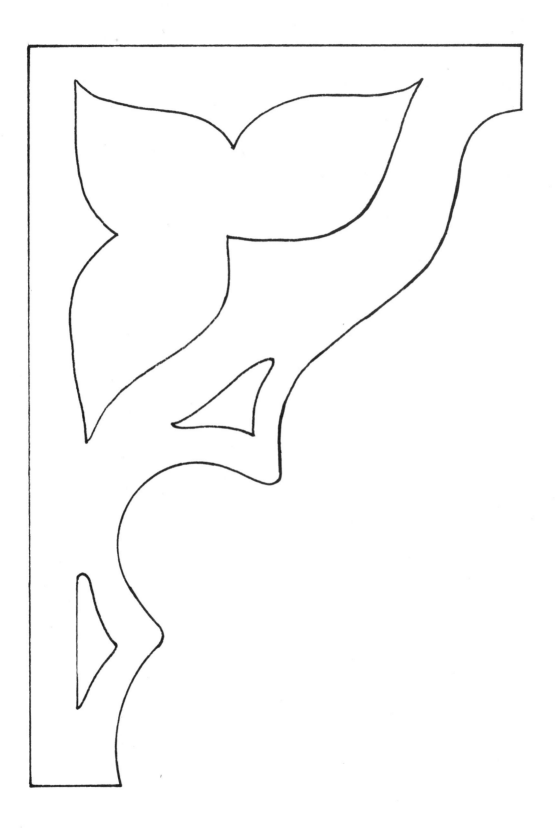

167

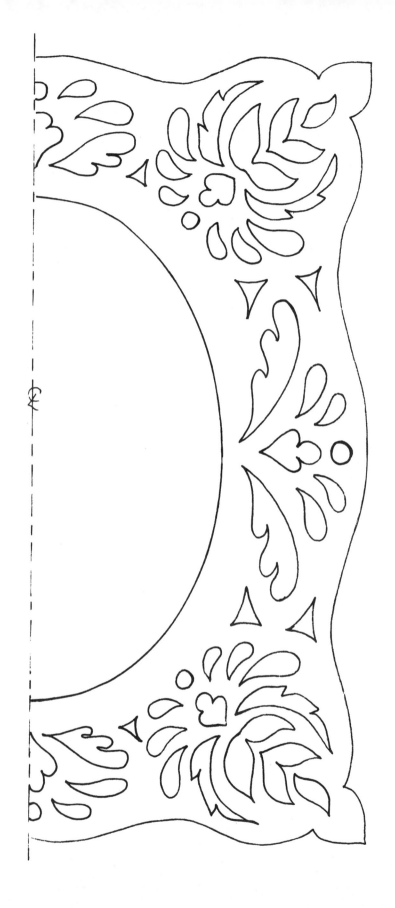

This pattern is half-size.
The frame opening is 4 × 5.

This fretwork shelf is made with ⅜-inch material.

BRACKET

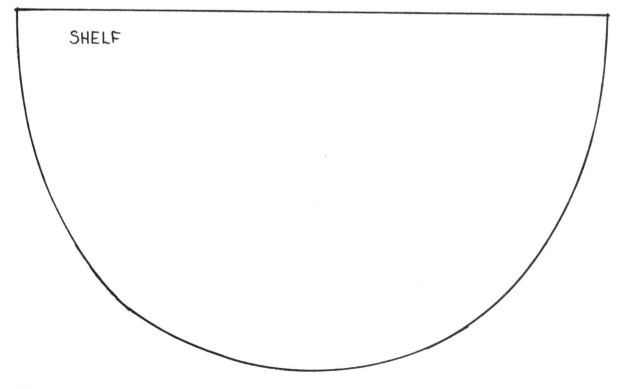

SHELF

174

SHELF

BRACKET

SHELF

CORNER SHELF

This corner shelf is made with ¼-inch plywood.

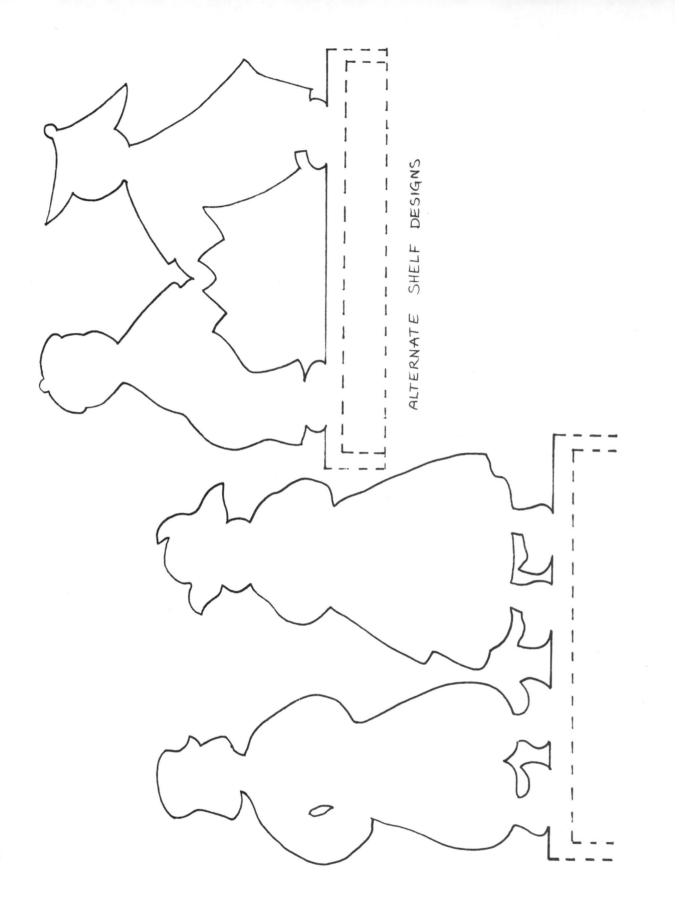

ALTERNATE SHELF DESIGNS

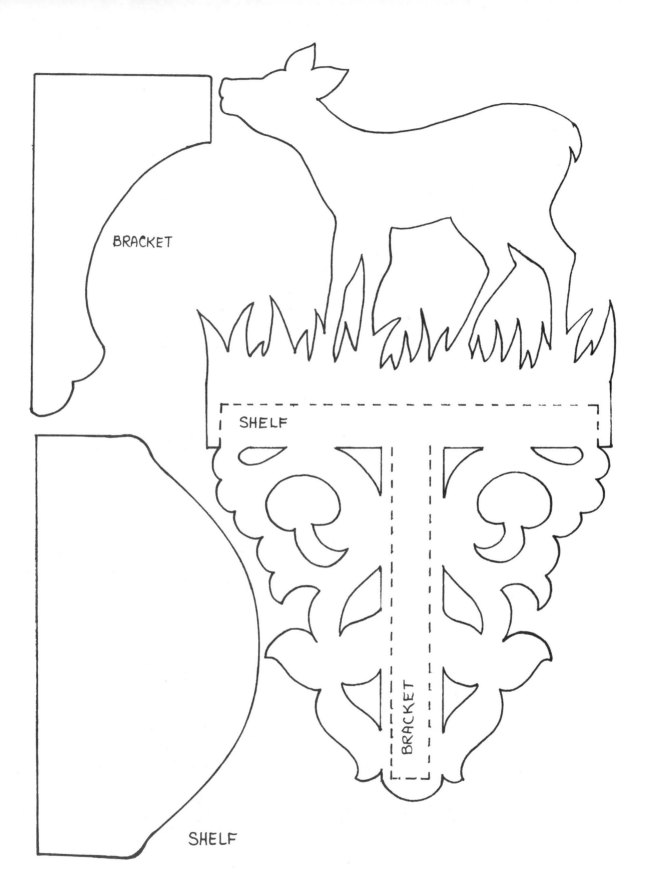

BRACKET

SHELF

BRACKET

SHELF

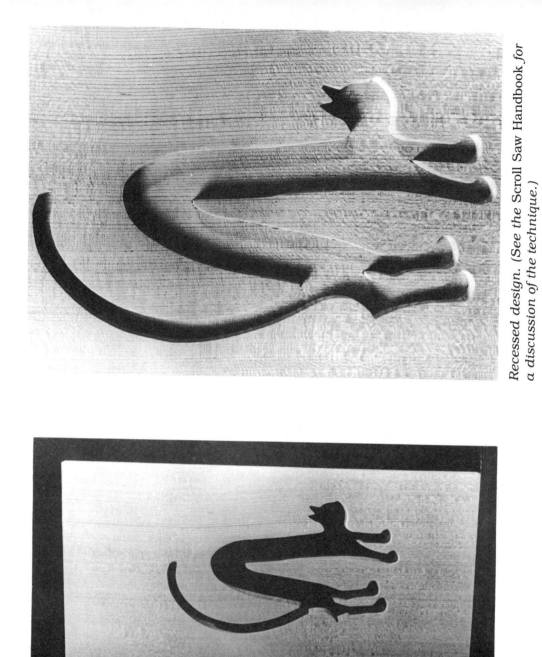

Recessed design. (See the Scroll Saw Handbook for a discussion of the technique.)

Simple cutout.

Simple silhouette sawn in a slab.

Designs in relief. (See the Scroll Saw Handbook for a discussion of the technique.)

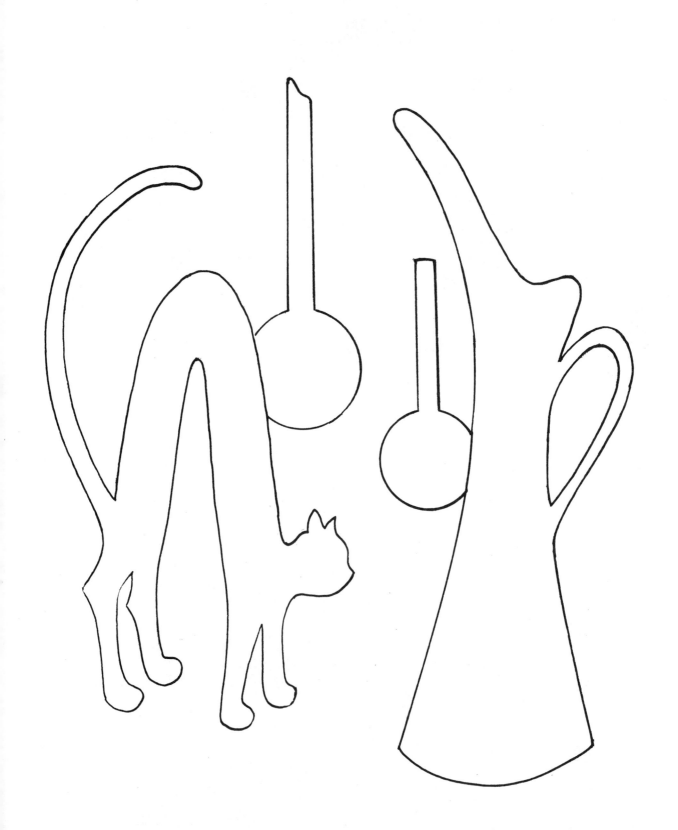

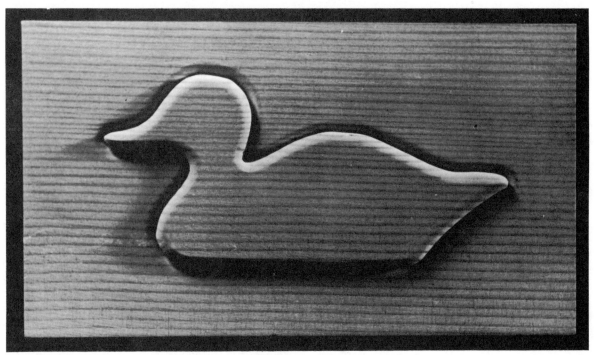

Simple line work, cut, rounded, and reinserted.

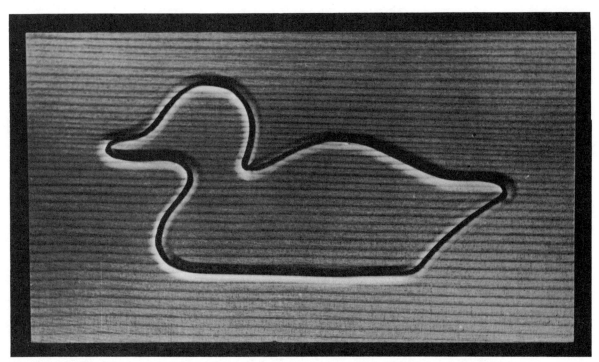

The same idea, but inserted in relief. (See the Scroll Saw Handbook *for more information.)*

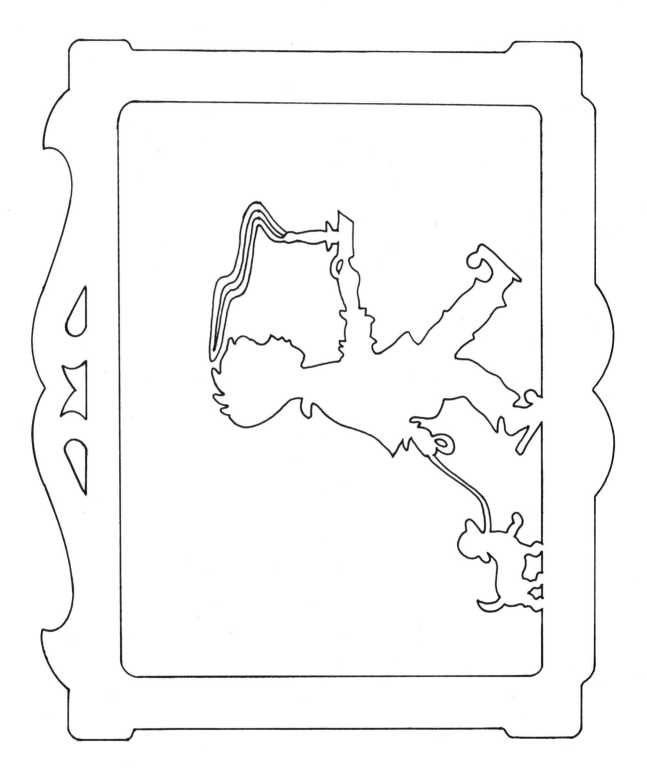

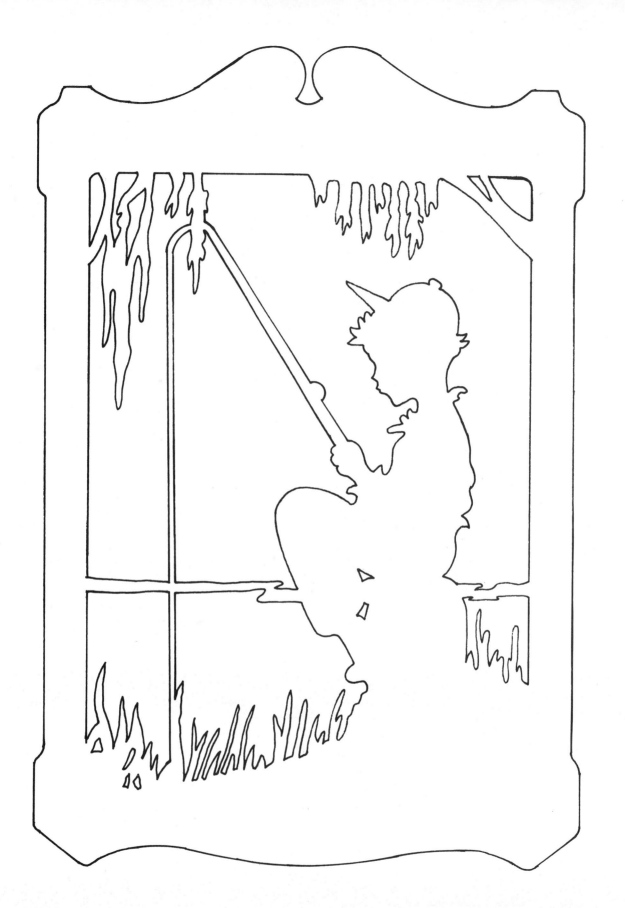

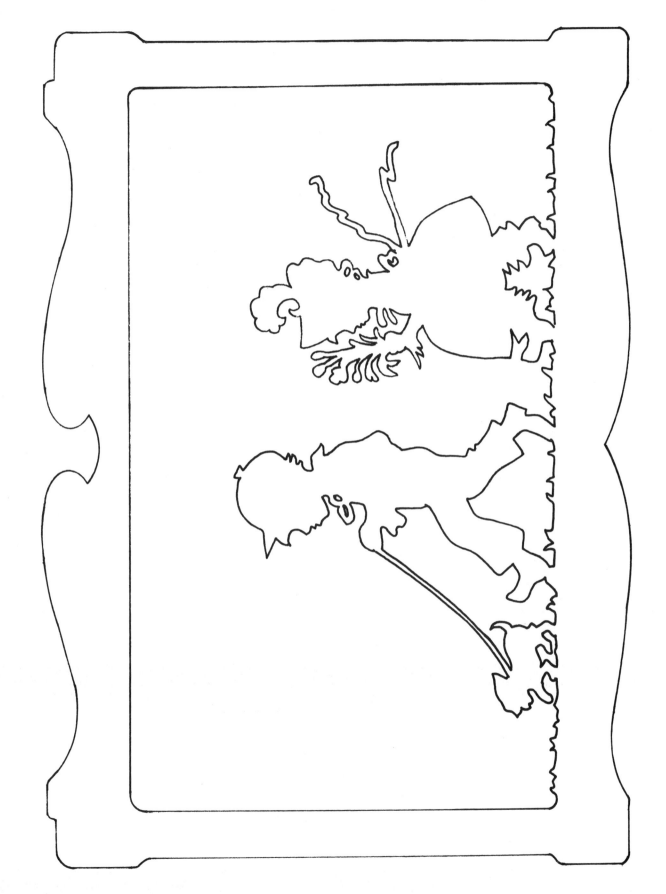

Marquetry/Inlays

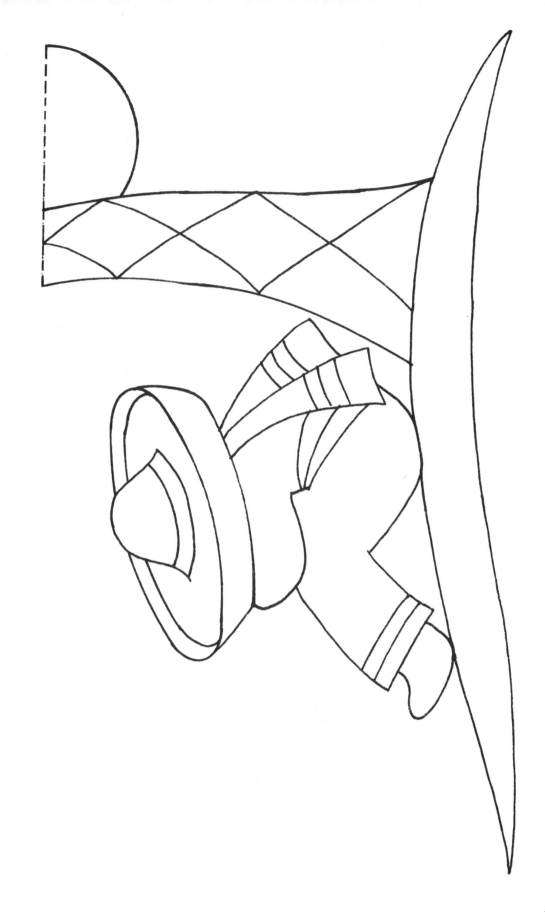

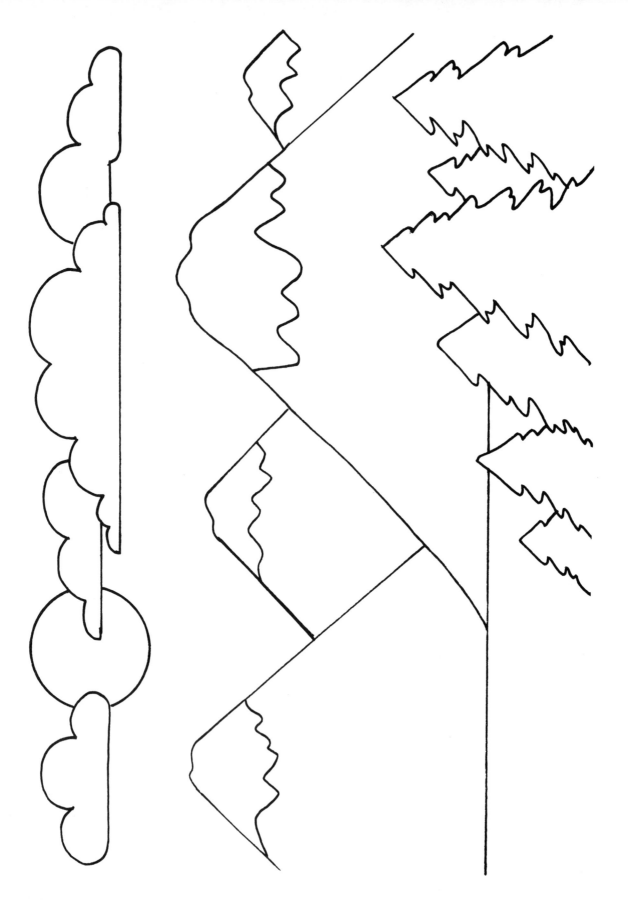

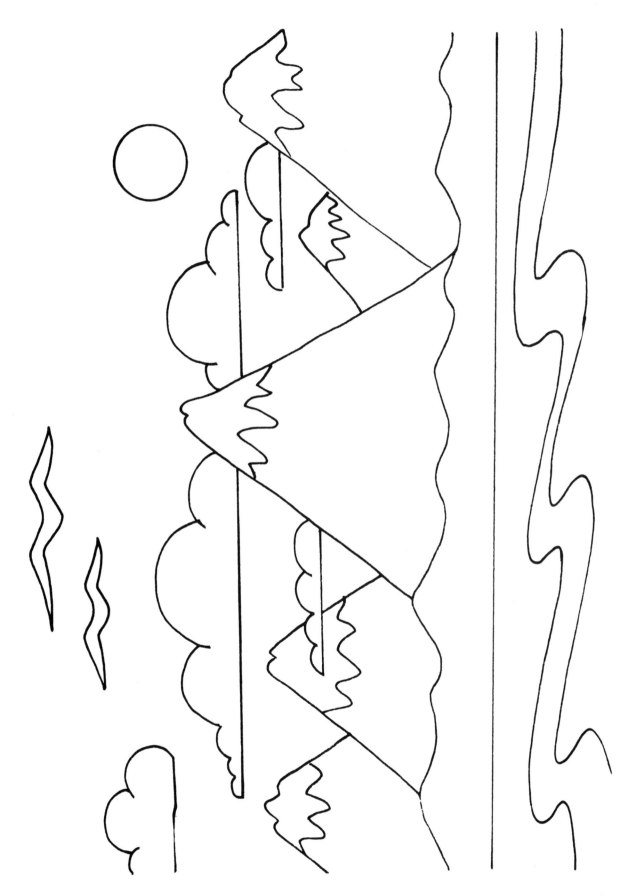

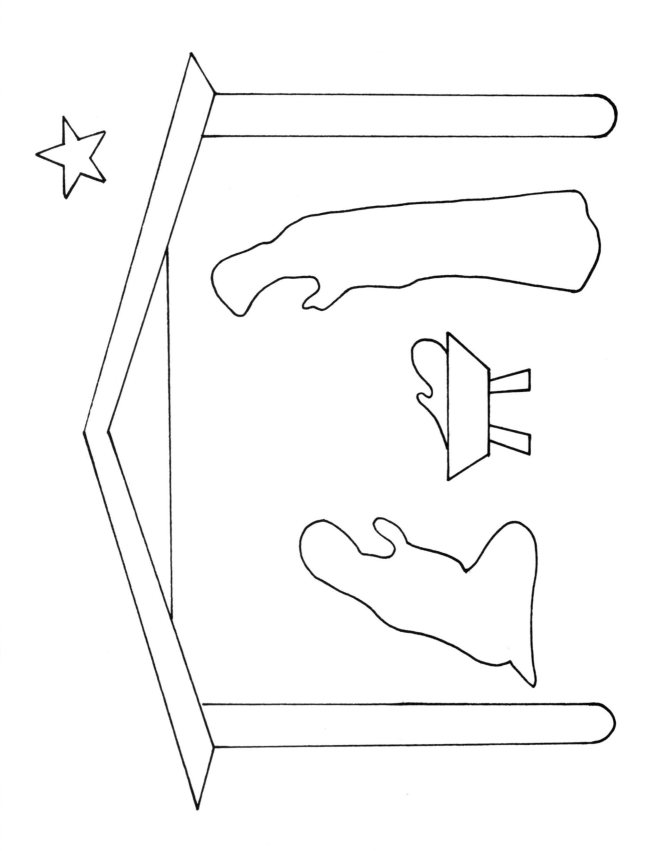

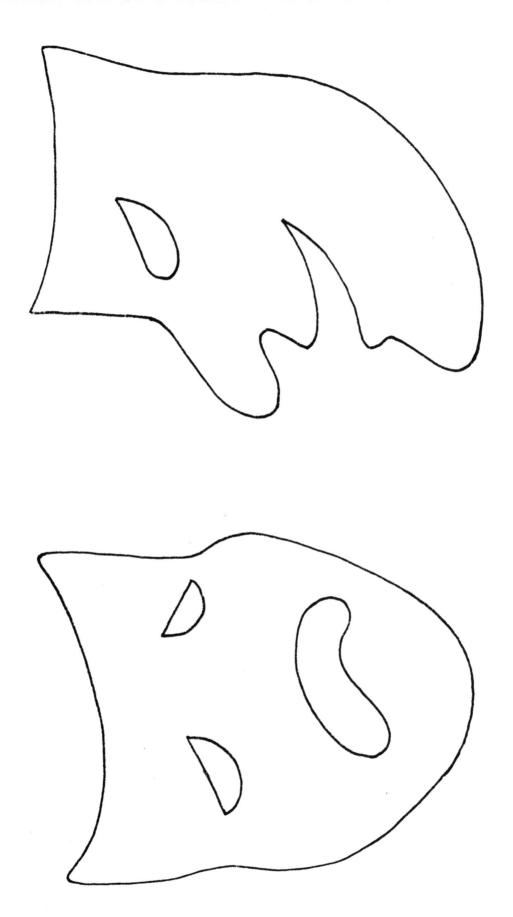

Lamp Assembly

Hanging hex lamps (above and below).

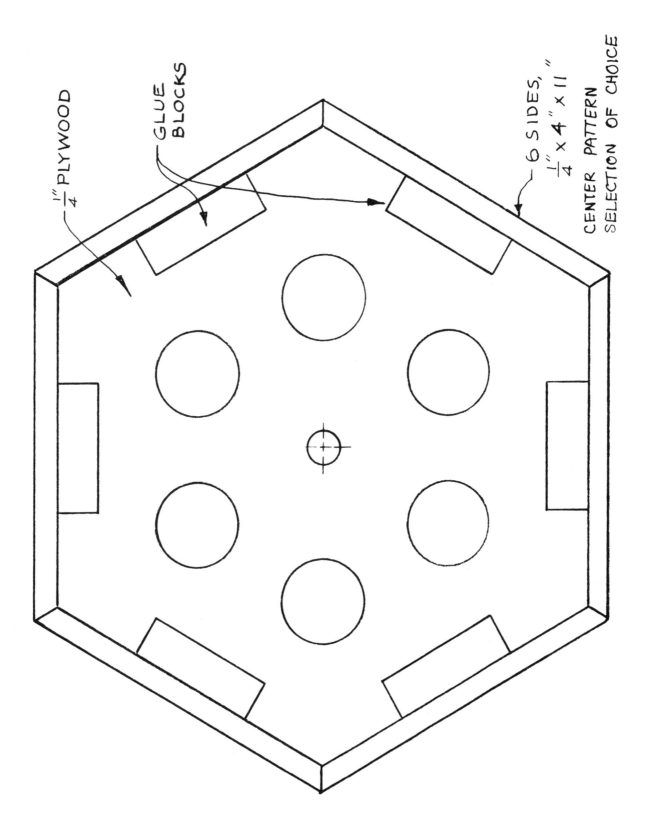

GLUE
BLOCKS

$\frac{1''}{4}$ PLYWOOD

6 SIDES,
$\frac{1''}{4} \times 4'' \times 11''$

CENTER PATTERN
SELECTION OF CHOICE

211

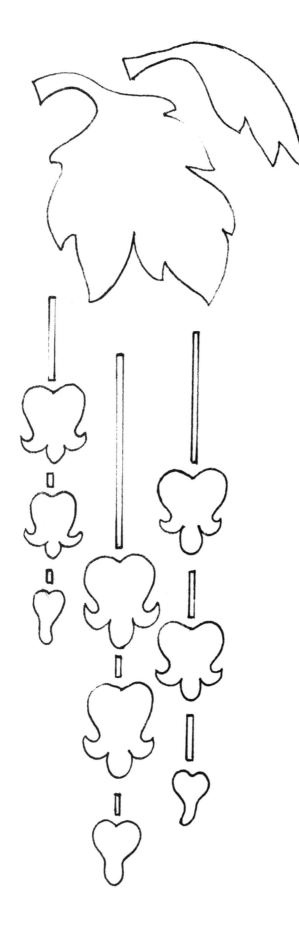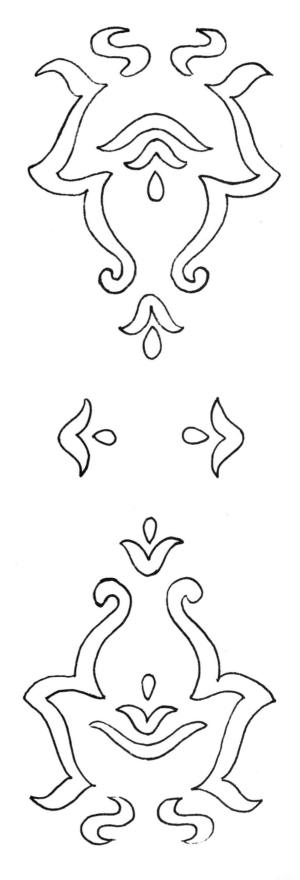

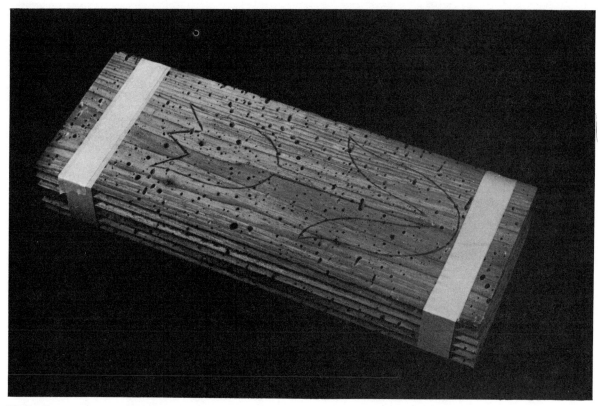

With the pattern centered in sized stock with 60 degree edges, stack the boards together for multiple sawing.

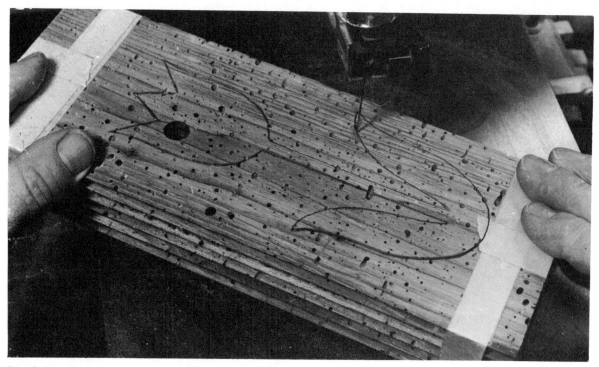

Stack sawing is a process in which all six sides are cut at one time.

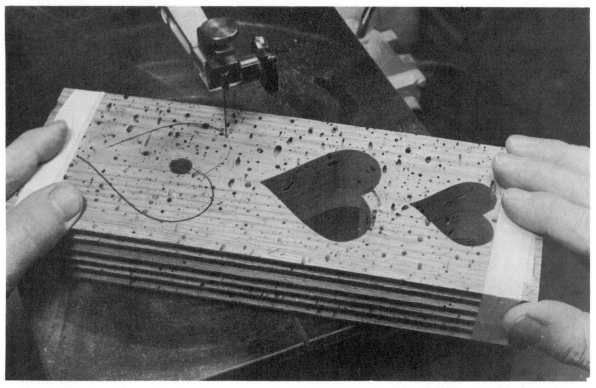

Stack sawing for another lamp.

Tape all six pieces together on the face side.

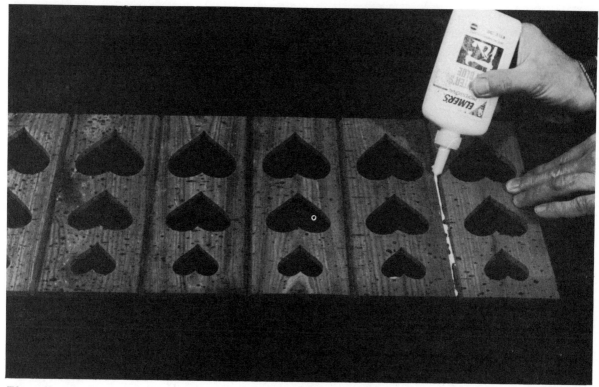

Flip all taped pieces over and spread glue in the "V" openings.

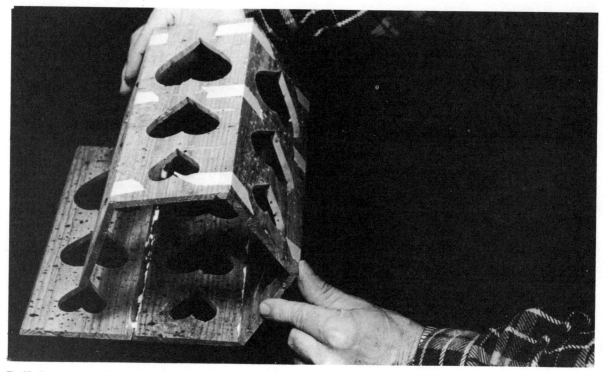

Pull the assembly together. The tape acts as a hinge and clamp.

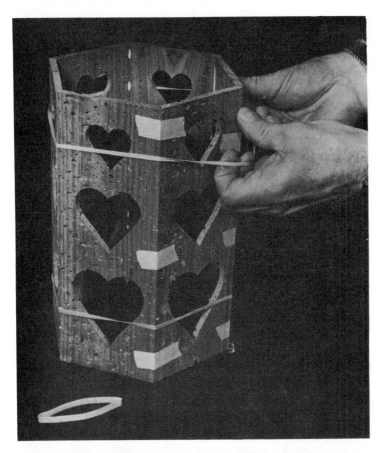

A few heavy rubber bands provide the clamping pressure.

The hex top is secured with triangular glue blocks.

Compound Sawing

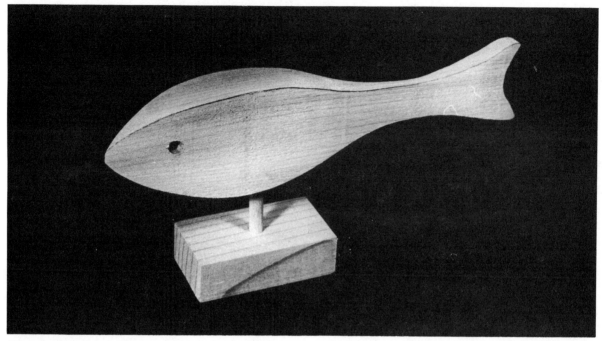

Simple fish formed by compound sawing.

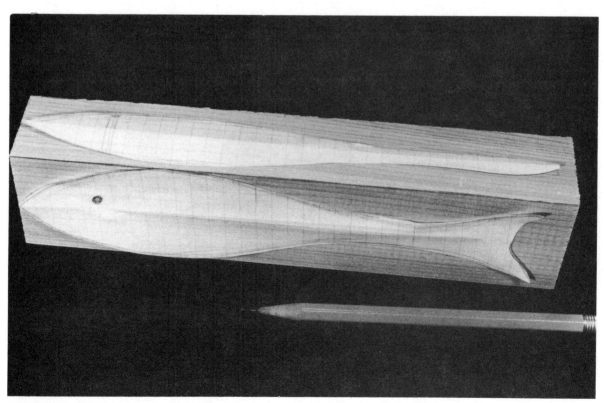

Transfer patterns to top and side surfaces.

Saw top-view shape first.

Tape all cuttings back together and cut out the side profile shape.

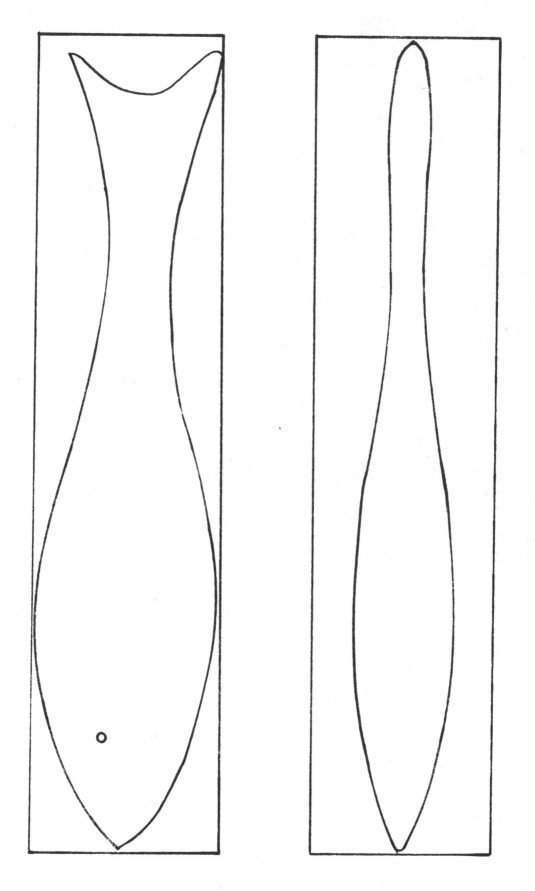

Compound-sawn tulip.

This weed holder and wood candle were made when a heart design was compound-sawn through. This candle is the replacement type used in food warmers that comes in a 1½-inch-diameter metal cup that's ¾ inch high.

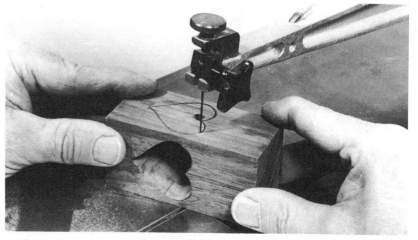

Completing the second heart cutout when compound-sawing.

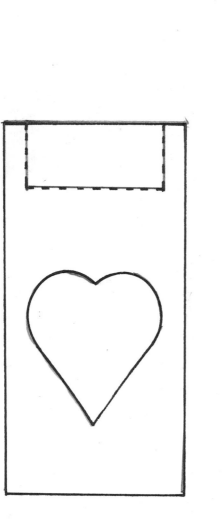
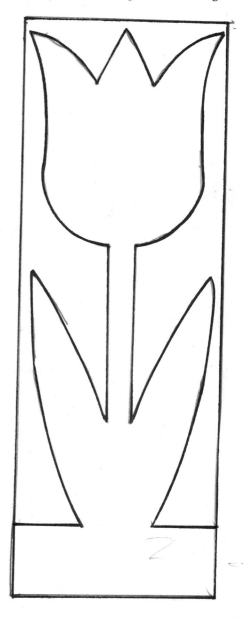

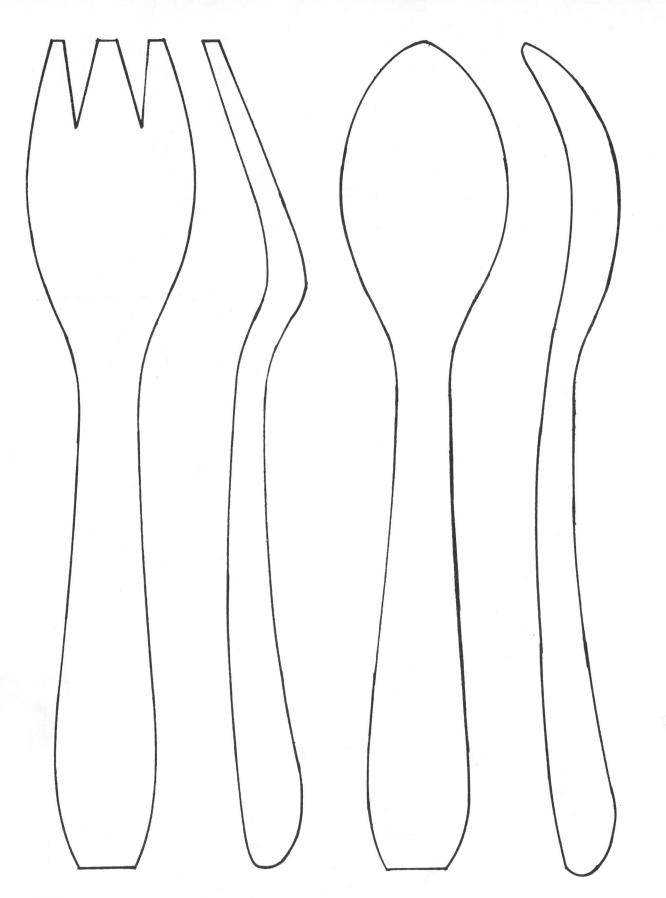

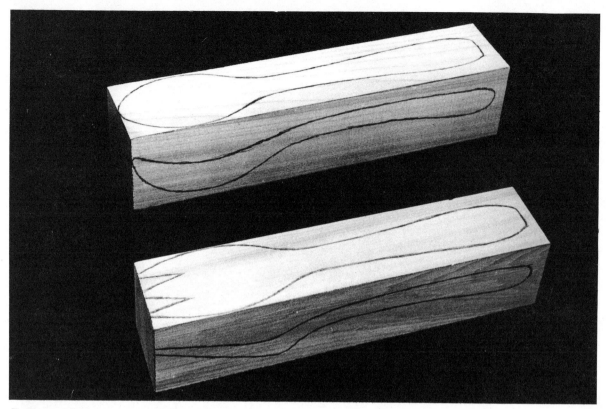

Patterns drawn on stock for compound-sawing of a salad, fork, and spoon project.

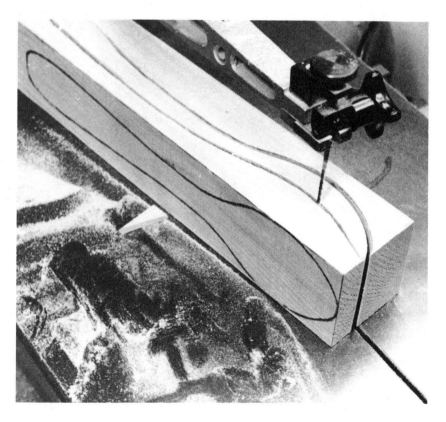

Sawing the side-view profile first.

Signboards

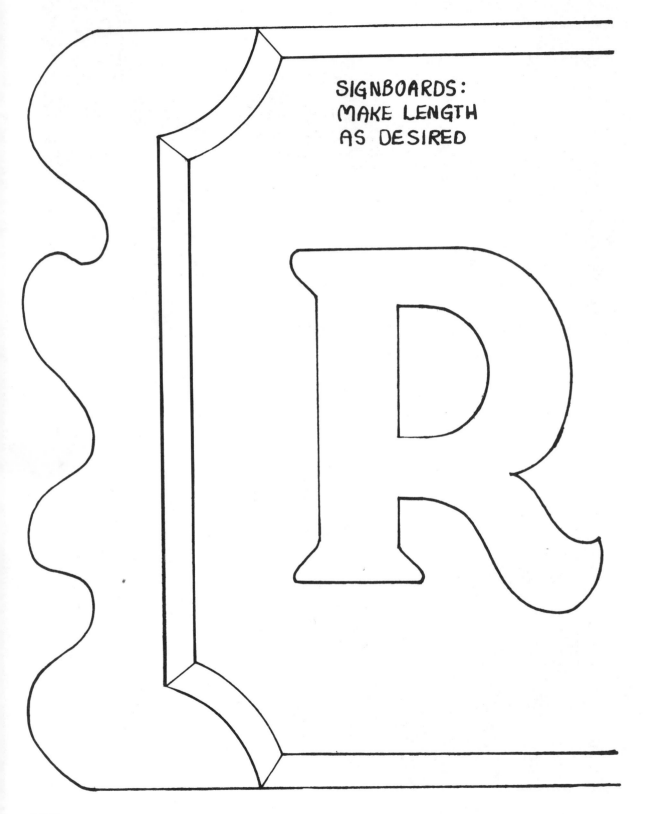

SIGNBOARDS:
MAKE LENGTH
AS DESIRED

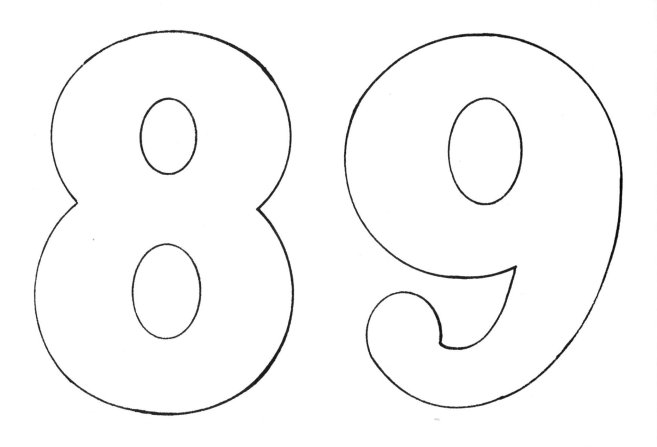

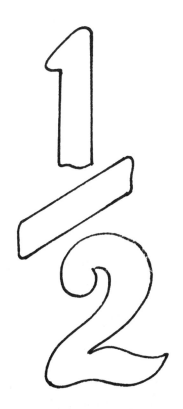

231

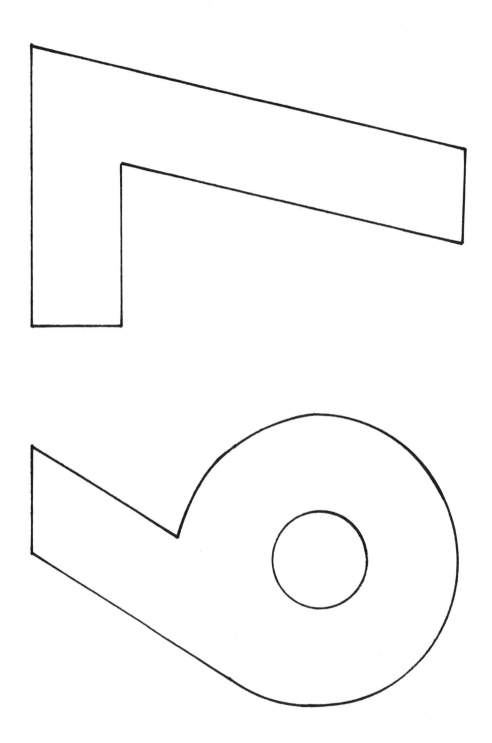

233

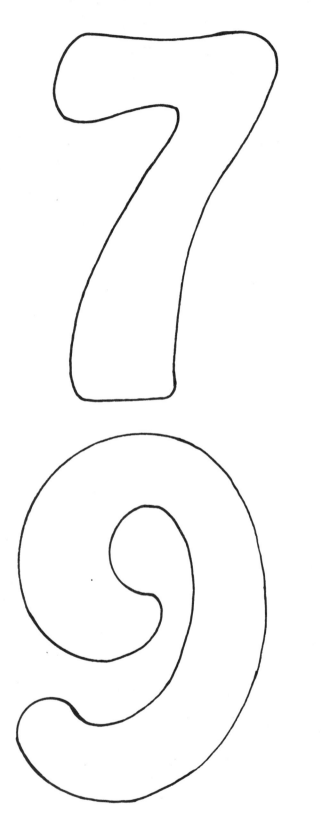
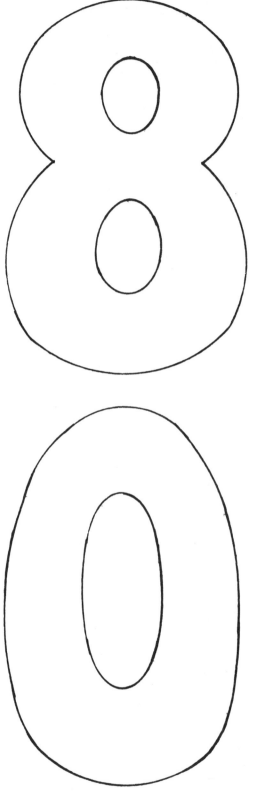

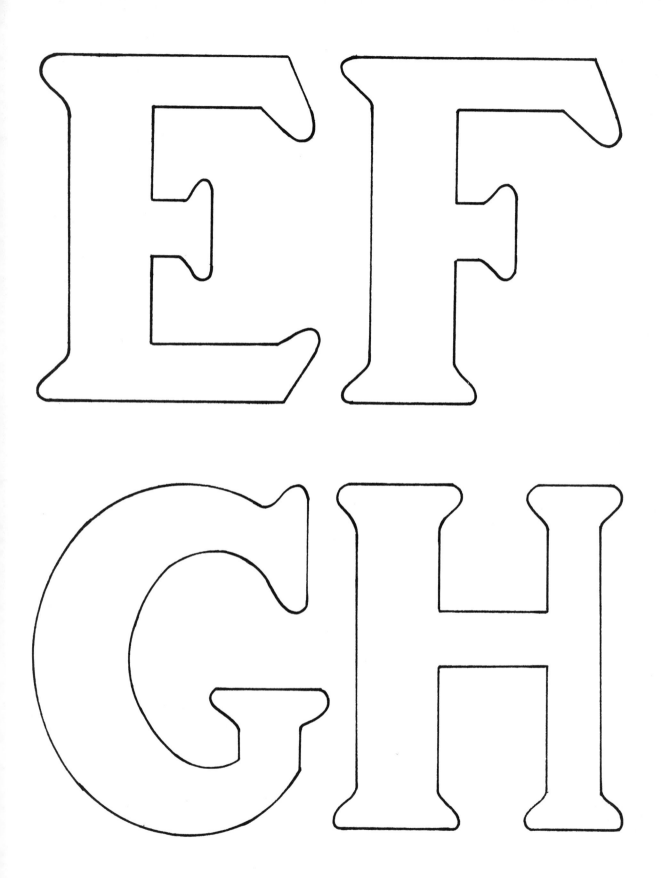

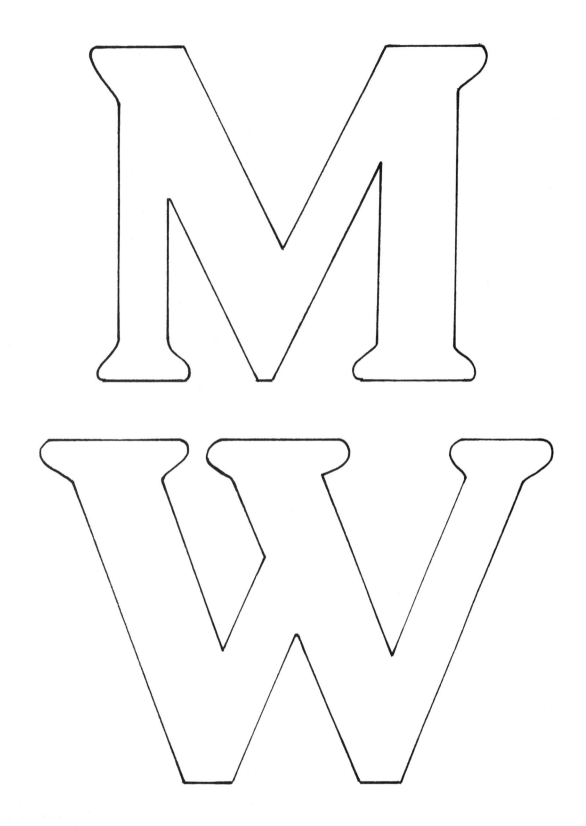

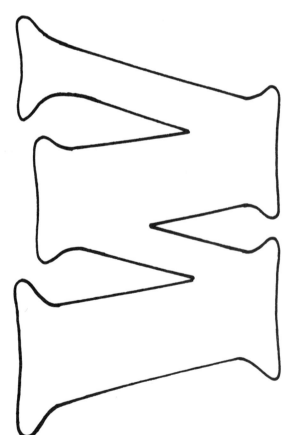

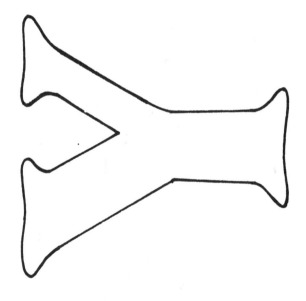

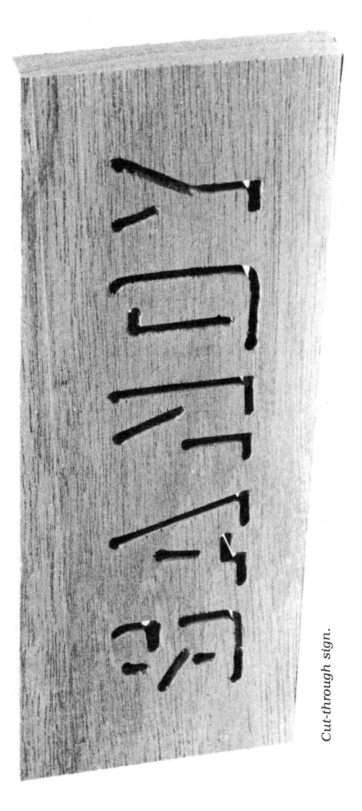

Cut-through sign.

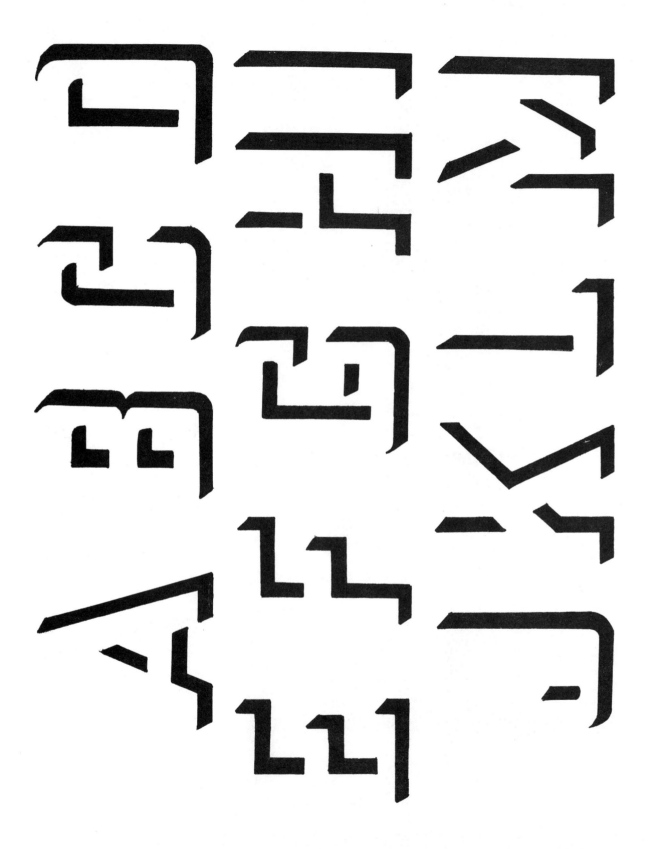

252

253

ABOUT THE AUTHORS

Patrick Spielman's love of wood began when, as a child, he transformed fruit crates into toys. Now this prolific and innovative woodworker is respected worldwide as a teacher and author.

His most famous contribution to the woodworking field has been his perfection of a method to season green wood with polyethylene glycol 1000 (PEG). He went on to invent, manufacture, and distribute the PEG-Thermovat chemical seasoning system.

During his many years as shop instructor in Wisconsin, Spielman published manuals, teaching guides, and more than 14 popular books, including *Modern Wood Technology*, a college text. He also wrote six educational series on wood technology, tool use, processing techniques, design, and wood-product planning.

Author of the best-selling *Router Handbook* (over 200,000 copies sold), Spielman has served as editorial consultant to a professional magazine, and his products, techniques, and many books have been featured in numerous periodicals.

This pioneer of new ideas and inventor of countless jigs, fixtures, and designs used throughout the world is a unique combination of expert woodworker and brilliant teacher—all of which endear him to his many readers and to his publisher.

At Spielmans Wood Works in the woods of northern Door County, Wisconsin, he and his family create and sell some of the most durable and popular furniture products and designs available.

As both a buyer of wood products and the creator of Spielmans Wood Works Gift Shop and Gallery, Patricia Spielman ("Mrs. Pat") plays an invaluable part in the success of Spielmans Wood Works—and is well respected for her discerning eye for design and natural artistic ability.

Should you wish to write Pat or Patricia, please forward your letters to Sterling Publishing Company.

CHARLES NURNBERG
STERLING PUBLISHING COMPANY

CURRENT BOOKS BY PATRICK SPIELMAN

Alphabets and Designs for Wood Signs. 50 alphabet patterns, plans for many decorative designs, the latest on hand carving, routing, cutouts, and sandblasting. Pricing data. Photo gallery (4 pages in color) of wood signs by professionals from across the U.S. Over 200 illustrations. 128 pages.

Carving Large Birds. Spielman and renowned carver Bill Dehos show how to carve a spectacular array of large birds. All the tools and basic techniques used are discussed in depth, and hundreds of photos, illustrations, and patterns are provided for carving graceful swans, majestic eagles, comical-looking penguins, and dozens of other birds. 16 pages in full color. 224 pages.

Gluing and Clamping. A thorough, up-to-date examination of one of the most critical steps in woodworking. Spielman explores the features of every type of glue—from traditional animal-hide glues to the newest epoxies—the clamps and tools needed, the bonding properties of different wood species, safety tips, and all techniques from edge-to-edge and end-to-end gluing to applying plastic laminates. Also included is a glossary of terms. Over 500 illustrations. 256 pages.

Making Country-Rustic Furniture. Hundreds of photos, patterns, and detailed scaled drawings reveal construction methods, woodworking techniques, and Spielman's professional secrets for making indoor and outdoor furniture in the distinctly attractive Country-Rustic style. Covered are all aspects of furniture making from choosing the best wood for the job to texturing smooth boards. Among the dozens of projects are mailboxes, cabinets, shelves, coffee tables, weather vanes, doors, panelling, plant stands and many more durable and economical pieces. 400 illustrations. 4 pages in full color. 164 pages.

Making Wood Decoys. A clear step-by-step approach to the basics of decoy carving. This book is abundantly illustrated with closeup photos for designing, selecting, and obtaining woods; tools; feather detailing; painting; and finishing of decorative and working decoys. Six different professional decoy artists are featured. Photo gallery (4 pages in full color) along with numerous detailed plans for various popular decoys. 160 pages.

Making Wood Signs. Designing, selecting woods, tools, and every process through finishing is clearly covered. Hand-carved, power-carved, routed, and sandblasted processes in small to huge signs are presented. Foolproof guides for professional letters and ornaments. Hundreds of photos (4 pages in full color). Lists sources for supplies and special tooling. 144 pages.

Realistic Decoys. Spielman and master carver Keith Bridenhagen reveal their successful techniques for carving, feather-texturing, painting, and finishing wood decoys. Details that you can't find elsewhere—anatomy, attitudes, markings, and the easy step-by-step approach to perfect delicate procedures—make this book invaluable. Includes listings for contests, shows, and sources of tools and supplies. 274 closeup photos, 28 in color. 224 pages.

Router Handbook. With nearly 600 illustrations of every conceivable bit, attachment, jig, and fixture, plus every possible operation, this definitive guide has revolutionized router applications. It begins with safety and maintenance tips, then forges ahead into all aspects of dovetailing, freehanding, advanced duplication, and more. Details for over 50 projects are included. 224 pages.

Scroll Saw Handbook. This companion volume to *Scroll Saw Pattern Book* covers the essentials of this versatile tool, including the basics (how scroll saws work, blades to use, etc.) and the advantages and disadvantages of the general types and specific brand name models available on the market. All cutting techniques are detailed, including compound and bevel sawing, making inlays, reliefs, and recesses, cutting metals and other nonwoods, and marquetry. There's even a section on transferring patterns to wood! Over 500 illustrations. 256 pages.

Working Green Wood with PEG. Covers every process for making beautiful, inexpensive projects from green wood without cracking, splitting, or warping. Hundreds of clear photos and drawings show every step from obtaining the raw wood through shaping, treating, and finishing your PEG-treated projects. 175 unusual project ideas. Lists supply sources. 160 pages.

INDEX